GANGS

OPPOSING VIEWPOINTS®

Other Books of Related Interest

GANGS

OPPOSING VIEWPOINTS®

Laura K. Egendorf, *Book Editor*

David L. Bender, *Publisher*
Bruno Leone, *Executive Editor*
Bonnie Szumski, *Editorial Director*
Stuart B. Miller, *Managing Editor*

OPPOSING
VIEWPOINTS®
SERIES

Greenhaven Press, Inc., San Diego, California

Cover photo: © Corbis

Library of Congress Cataloging-in-Publication Data

Gangs : opposing viewpoints / Laura K. Egendorf, book editor.
    p.   cm. — (Opposing viewpoints series)
   Includes bibliographical references and index.
   ISBN 0-7377-0509-4 (pbk. : alk. paper) —
ISBN 0-7377-0510-8 (lib. bdg. : alk. paper)
   1. Gangs—United States. 2. Violent crimes—United States.
3. Criminal justice, Administration of—United States.
I. Egendorf, Laura K., 1973–   . II. Opposing viewpoints series
(Unnumbered)

HV6439.U5 G364 2001
364.1'06'60973—dc21
                                                    00-029332
                                                    CIP

Greenhaven Press, Inc., P.O. Box 289009
San Diego, CA 92198-9009

"Congress shall make
no law...abridging the
freedom of speech, or of
the press."

First Amendment to the U.S. Constitution

The basic foundation of our democracy is the First
Amendment guarantee of freedom of expression. The
Opposing Viewpoints Series is dedicated to the
concept of this basic freedom and the idea that it is
more important to practice it than to enshrine it.

Contents

Why Consider Opposing Viewpoints?

"The only way in which a human being can make some approach to knowing the whole of a subject is by hearing what can be said about it by persons of every variety of opinion and studying all modes in which it can be looked at by every character of mind. No wise man ever acquired his wisdom in any mode but this."

John Stuart Mill

In our media-intensive culture it is not difficult to find differing opinions. Thousands of newspapers and magazines and dozens of radio and television talk shows resound with differing points of view. The difficulty lies in deciding which opinion to agree with and which "experts" seem the most credible. The more inundated we become with differing opinions and claims, the more essential it is to hone critical reading and thinking skills to evaluate these ideas. Opposing Viewpoints books address this problem directly by presenting stimulating debates that can be used to enhance and teach these skills. The varied opinions contained in each book examine many different aspects of a single issue. While examining these conveniently edited opposing views, readers can develop critical thinking skills such as the ability to compare and contrast authors' credibility, facts, argumentation styles, use of persuasive techniques, and other stylistic tools. In short, the Opposing Viewpoints Series is an ideal way to attain the higher-level thinking and reading skills so essential in a culture of diverse and contradictory opinions.

In addition to providing a tool for critical thinking, Opposing Viewpoints books challenge readers to question their own strongly held opinions and assumptions. Most people form their opinions on the basis of upbringing, peer pressure, and personal, cultural, or professional bias. By reading carefully balanced opposing views, readers must directly confront new ideas as well as the opinions of

those with whom they disagree. This is not to simplisti-
cally argue that everyone who reads opposing views
will—or should—change his or her opinion. Instead, the
series enhances readers' understanding of their own views
by encouraging confrontation with opposing ideas. Careful examination of others' views can lead to the readers'
understanding of the logical inconsistencies in their own
opinions, perspective on why they hold an opinion, and
the consideration of the possibility that their opinion requires further evaluation.

Evaluating Other Opinions

To ensure that this type of examination occurs, Opposing
Viewpoints books present all types of opinions. Prominent
spokespeople on different sides of each issue as well as well-
known professionals from many disciplines challenge the
reader. An additional goal of the series is to provide a forum
for other, less known, or even unpopular viewpoints. The
opinion of an ordinary person who has had to make the decision to cut off life support from a terminally ill relative,
for example, may be just as valuable and provide just as
much insight as a medical ethicist's professional opinion.
The editors have two additional purposes in including these
less known views. One, the editors encourage readers to respect others' opinions—even when not enhanced by professional credibility. It is only by reading or listening to and
objectively evaluating others' ideas that one can determine
whether they are worthy of consideration. Two, the inclu-
sion of such viewpoints encourages the important critical
thinking skill of objectively evaluating an author's credentials and bias. This evaluation will illuminate an author's
reasons for taking a particular stance on an issue and will
aid in readers' evaluation of the author's ideas.

As series editors of the Opposing Viewpoints Series, it is
our hope that these books will give readers a deeper understanding of the issues debated and an appreciation of the
complexity of even seemingly simple issues when good and
honest people disagree. This awareness is particularly important in a democratic society such as ours in which people
enter into public debate to determine the common good.

Those with whom one disagrees should not be regarded as enemies but rather as people whose views deserve careful examination and may shed light on one's own.

Thomas Jefferson once said that "difference of opinion leads to inquiry, and inquiry to truth." Jefferson, a broadly educated man, argued that "if a nation expects to be ignorant and free . . . it expects what never was and never will be." As individuals and as a nation, it is imperative that we consider the opinions of others and examine them with skill and discernment. The Opposing Viewpoints Series is intended to help readers achieve this goal.

David L. Bender & Bruno Leone,
Series Editors

Greenhaven Press anthologies primarily consist of previously published material taken from a variety of sources, including periodicals, books, scholarly journals, newspapers, government documents, and position papers from private and public organizations. These original sources are often edited for length and to ensure their accessibility for a young adult audience. The anthology editors also change the original titles of these works in order to clearly present the main thesis of each viewpoint and to explicitly indicate the opinion presented in the viewpoint. These alterations are made in consideration of both the reading and comprehension levels of a young adult audience. Every effort is made to ensure that Greenhaven Press accurately reflects the original intent of the authors included in this anthology.

Introduction

"Two factors mark the major differentiation between earlier violent gangs and today's violent gangs: the intensified commerce of drugs and the violence that surrounds the drug business, and the enormous increase in the availability of lethal automatic weapons that are used in gang murders."

—Lewis Yablonsky, Gangsters: Fifty Years of Madness, Drugs, and Death on the Streets of America

Gangs are not a new problem in the United States; they have existed in New York and other eastern cities for more than two hundred years. An examination of gang life in 1940s and 1950s New York and 1960s and 1970s Los Angeles helps explain the development of late twentieth-century gangs—gangs that scholars argue are far more violent than their mid-century predecessors.

Eric C. Schneider explored 1940s and 1950s gang life in his book *Vampires, Dragons, and Egyptian Gangs: Youth Gangs in Postwar New York*. Unlike the Italian, Irish, and Jewish gangs of the early twentieth century, the gangs formed during and after World War II were increasingly non-European in origin. Among these gangs were the Rainbows and Hancocks (white gangs), the Chancellors and Negro Sabres (African American gangs) and the Viceroys and Latin Gents (Puerto Rican gangs). The influx of Puerto Rican and African American gangs into white neighborhoods sometimes led to violent conflicts between the newcomers and white gangs. Schneider observes that while serious injuries and murder did occasionally occur as a result of gang skirmishes in the early 1940s, "few gangs had access to real weapons, and when clashes occurred, nervous adolescents and single-shot weapons kept casualties low." He also notes that gangs were able to keep violence to a relative minimum by "[imposing] their own order and codes for behavior." These codes—which were not always observed—included establishing neutral territory and not attacking adults.

Although stabbings and hand-to-hand violence remained

the primary methods of fighting, guns became easier to obtain in the postwar years, and consequently, New York gangs became more violent. According to Schneider, the homicide rate for adolescents nearly tripled between 1940 and 1946, increasing from 1.28 deaths per 100,000 to 3.45 deaths per 100,000. The number of adolescents arrested for murder increased from 34 arrests in 1940 to 88 arrests in 1946. By 1947, the gang problem prompted the formation of the New York City Youth Board, which sent social workers into the streets to gather information about and develop relationships with gangs. While the Youth Board, which was disbanded in 1976, did obtain a considerable amount of data about gangs, it did not solve the gang problem.

Like New York City, Los Angeles also has a lengthy gang history. The Los Angeles street gangs of the 1940s through the mid-1960s sometimes had violent confrontations but murders were rare. According to Alejandro A. Alonso, a professor at Santa Monica City College, most fights were hand-to-hand, though chains and bats were sometimes used. However, things began to change after the August 1965 Watts riots. African Americans, enraged by social injustice, rioted in the Watts neighborhood in southwestern Los Angeles; thirty-four people died and more than one thousand were injured. Some Los Angeles gangs, including the Gladiators, Slausons, and Rebel Rousers, formed an alliance and participated in the riots. Ironically, these gangs' participation helped usher in new groups that were more political and less likely to participate in traditional gang confrontation.

Two of these post-Watts organizations were the Black Panthers (a black militant party, founded in 1966 by Huey Newton and Bobby Seale) and the Brown Berets (formed in 1967 by a group of Hispanic students). Both groups replaced gang violence with social action; they established free health clinics, and the Black Panthers also developed free breakfast programs for children. The Black Panthers and Brown Berets protested against what they felt was racism and harassment by the police. Although intra-gang violence had been muted, conflicts with the police were often deadly.

While gang violence might have eased somewhat in the late 1960s and early 1970s, that era was not wholly peaceful, as it was during this period when the two most notorious Los Angeles gangs, the Crips and the Bloods, were formed. Raymond Johnson, Stanley Williams, and Jamiel Barnes founded the Crips—originally named the Avenue Cribs—in 1969. The Bloods were formed in 1972, following a conflict that summer between the Crips and another gang, the Pirus. The Pirus and other gangs that had fought with the Crips unified to become the Bloods.

Gang violence increased significantly in the 1980s, which is considered by experts to be the beginning of the contemporary gang era. Rather than relying on switchblades or hand-to-hand fighting, gang members were now using guns and automatic weapons to commit crimes. These weapons have significantly increased the number of gang-related homicides. Innocent bystanders are also more likely to be killed when these guns are used in a drive-by shooting. Lewis Yablonsky, an emeritus professor of criminology at California State University at Northridge, writes: "Only about 50 percent of gang-related murders hit the target of enemy gangsters." Another major difference between gangs past and present is the explosion of the illegal drug market. The gangs of the 1940s to 1970s were largely uninvolved in the drug trade and more likely to hold regular jobs. By the 1980s, however, drug dealing had become a more prevalent income source. Schneider explains that lenient punishments for adolescent drug dealers, the development of crack in the 1980s, and an expanding market "converged to create an inner-city 'enterprise zone' based on illegal drugs."

Although New York and Los Angeles have a long gang history, gangs are not just a city problem. Gangs have entered the suburbs and rural areas as well, making modern gangs an issue that can affect almost anybody. In *Gangs: Opposing Viewpoints*, the authors analyze modern gangs in these chapters: What Factors Influence Gang Behavior? How Widespread Is the Problem of Gangs? Can the Criminal Justice System Reduce Gang Violence? How Can Society End the Threat of Gangs? In those chapters, the authors debate how to respond to the problems posed by the growing gang presence.

CHAPTER 1

What Factors Influence Gang Behavior?

Chapter Preface

In his paper "Youth Gangs: An Overview," James C. Howell notes that one of the risk factors for youth gang membership is "barriers to and lack of social and economic opportunities." While some people join gangs to impress friends or escape abusive households, others join because they live in poor urban neighborhoods and believe that gang life offers the best avenue for economic stability.

The unemployment rate in inner cities in November 1999 was higher than the national average of 4.1 percent, according to the Bureau of Labor Statistics. The figure, as reported by the BLS, is especially high for African American teenagers—their unemployment rate in November 1999 was 28.9 percent, compared to 12.1 percent for whites between the ages of sixteen and nineteen. These jobs that do exist are in the suburbs and thus inaccessible to urban youth because they are outside the reach of public transportation. Many of the jobs also require skills that are not taught at inadequate urban schools. Francine Garcia-Hallcom, a professor who has researched Los Angeles street gangs, explains the circumstances facing at-risk youth: "Teens who graduate from ghetto schools do not know enough to get even a minimal 9 to 5 office job, and more often than not—any kind of job at all."

However, other people question whether the difficulty at-risk youth have finding legitimate jobs is a factor in gang participation. In his review of William Julius Wilson's book *When Work Disappears: The World of the New Urban Poor*, Glenn C. Loury contends that inner-city teenagers might not turn away from gang violence, even if more jobs are provided. According to Loury, negative attitudes toward work and responsibility make "too many ghetto dwellers . . . unfit for work." He adds: "The fact that most criminals are unemployed is not sufficient proof that unstable ghetto youths will prefer minimum-wage employment to entry-level positions in the crack trade."

While poverty may lead some teens to join gangs, most teens in difficult circumstances do not join gangs. In the following chapter, the authors debate which factors lead some youth to participate in gang life.

"Most gangsters come from dysfunctional families with brutal or absentee fathers."

Poor Parenting Causes Some Children to Join Gangs

Lewis Yablonsky

In the following viewpoint, Lewis Yablonsky contends that children who grow up in abusive and dysfunctional homes or who have parents who abuse drugs are more likely to participate in gang violence than children who have nurturing parents. According to Yablonsky, substance-abusing parents are self-centered and unable to teach their children how to be caring and compassionate. In addition, he asserts that abused or neglected children develop low self-esteem and have little regard for their well-being, which leads to self-destructive behavior such as joining gangs. Yablonsky is the author of *Gangsters: Fifty Years of Madness, Drugs, and Death on the Streets of America*, from which this viewpoint is excerpted.

As you read, consider the following questions:

1. What do youth learn from effective adult role models, in Yablonsky's opinion?
2. What traits does a child raised in a substance-abusing family typically display, as stated by Yablonsky?
3. According to the author, what are the four basic forms of discipline?

It is of value to analyze the causal factors that produces the sociopathic gangster. The following analysis reveals some of the family and parental socialization factors that help to create the gangster's sociopathic personality.

An adequate social self develops from a consistent pattern of interaction with rational adult parents in a normative family socialization process. Effective adult role models, especially two parents, help a youth learn social feelings of love, compassion, and sympathy. This concept of adequate self-emergence through constructive social interaction with others, especially parents, is grounded in the theoretical and research findings of a number of social psychologists.

For example, sociologist G.H. Mead, on the issue of the proper personality development that results from effective parental socialization of a child, asserts,

> The self arises in conduct when the individual becomes a social object in experience to himself. This takes place when the individual assumes the attitude or uses the gestures which another individual (usually his parents) would use. Through socialization, the child gradually becomes a social being. The self thus has its origin in communication and in taking the role of the other.

Social psychologist Harry Stack Sullivan perceived the self as being made up of what he calls "reflected appraisals." According to Sullivan,

> The child lacks equipment and experience necessary for a careful and unclouded evaluation of himself. The only guides he has are those of the significant adults or others who take care of him and treat him with compassion. The child thus experiences and appraises himself in accordance with the reactions of parents and others close to him. By facial expressions, gestures, words, and deeds, they convey to him the attitudes they hold toward him, their regard for him or lack of it.

In brief, a set of positive sympathetic responses by socializing agents, usually the child's parents, are necessary for adequate self-growth. This component is generally absent in the development of youths who become sociopathic gangsters.

The Missing Ingredient

The basic ingredient, missing in most sociopathic gangster's socialization, is a loving parent or adult. Based on extensive research, Joan and William McCord assert,

> Because the rejected child does not love his parents and they do not love him, no identification takes place. Nor does the rejected child feel the loss of love—a love which he never had—when he violates moral restriction. Without love from an adult socializing agent, the psychopath remains asocial.

Psychologists Edwin Megargee and Roy Golden carried out extensive research cross-comparing psychopathic delinquent youths, including gangsters, with a control group of nondelinquent youths. Based on their research they concluded that sociopathic delinquents had a significantly poorer relation with their parents than nondelinquents; and the sociopathic delinquents had significantly more negative attitudes toward their mothers and their fathers than those of nondelinquents.

Dr. Marshall Cherkas, an eminent psychiatrist, in his thirty years of experience as a court psychiatrist interviewed several hundred delinquent sociopaths, including a number of gangsters. His conclusions about the origin of the sociopathic delinquent's personality summarizes the observations of other theorists on the subject. I concur with the following statement he presented to me in an interview on the causal context of the sociopath's early family life experience:

> Children are extremely dependent upon nurturing parents for life's sustenance as well as satisfaction and avoidance of pain. In the earliest phase of life, in their first year, infants maintain a highly narcissistic position in the world. Their sense of security, comfort, reality, and orientation is focused on their own primitive needs with little awareness and reality testing of the external world. As the normal infant develops, its security and comfort is reasonably assured. There occurs a natural attachment, awareness, and interest in "the Other." As the child matures, the dependency upon "the Other," its parents, diminishes, but the strength of the self is enhanced, and the child develops an awareness that its narcissistic needs are met through a cooperative, adaptive, and mutually supportive relationship to its parents and others. In other words, the child recognizes that even though its selfish (narcissistic) needs are extremely important, they can best be served by appropriately relating to other people, especially its parents.

> Infants whose needs are not adequately met because of the parents' own exaggerated narcissistic needs develop feelings of

mistrust, insecurity, and wariness about the capacities of their provider. In order to protect itself, the child may perform many tasks to gain attention, support, and interest from the parent. The child also begins to feel that it cannot trust others, and that its needs can only be met through self-interest. The child who cannot count on its own parents begins to become egocentric and therefore sociopathic in its behavior.

Based on my experience, I have determined that the basic reason for the sociopathic gangster's lack of trust noted by Cherkes and others is primarily a result of the physical, emotional, and sexual abuse that he has received from his parents in the context of his socialization process. The emotional abuse is often in the form of the absence of any socialization of the needs of the child or of outright abandonment.

The Consequences of Poor Parenting

The parental factor in the socialization of a gangster has several roots and implications. Children who are physically, sexually, or emotionally abused or abandoned by their parents develop low self-esteem and are more prone to commit acts of violence. They also denigrate themselves, feel worthless, and are less likely to care about what happens to them. These negative social-psychological forces contribute to the acting out of self-destructive behavior, including drug abuse and violent gangster behavior.

Most youths who become sociopathic gangsters have parents who are alcoholics or drug addicts. In extreme cases, at birth they are physiologically affected by being born to a mother who is an addicted crack-cocaine, heroin, or alcohol user. These children are sometimes born addicted and have severe physiological and psychological deficits.

As most research and my own observations over the years have revealed, substance abuse is an egocentric problem. The drug addict or alcoholic is consumed with the machinations of his or her habit. In a significant sense, whether or not the parents have a sociopathic personality, their behavior in the throes of their addiction is self-centered and consequently sociopathic in their relationship to their child. This form of parenting is not conducive to effectively socializing a child into a caring, compassionate, loving person. Children who are socialized in the chaotic world of a substance-abusing family tend to have a limited trust of others, become egocentric, and acompassionate. These sociopathic personality factors facilitate their participation in the violent gang. In brief, based on this varied research and its theoretical implications, it can be concluded that the proper and functional adult role models necessary for adequate socialization are usually absent from the social environment of youths who become gangsters.

Most gangsters come from dysfunctional families with brutal or absentee fathers. The negative adult role model that a youth growing up without a father may emulate is often the "ghetto hustler"—a fixture in the black hood. Malcolm X in his autobiography described this type of negative role model as follows:

> The most dangerous black man in America is the ghetto hustler. . . . The ghetto hustler is internally restrained by nothing. He has no religion, no concept of morality, no civic responsibility, no fear—nothing. This type of individual's hustle may be drugs, and he is often a father who has abandoned his son.

Ineffective Discipline and Physical Abuse

A significant factor in this cauldron of substance-abusing, negative parental impacts is related to ineffectual discipline. Essentially there are four basic forms of discipline in the socialization process of a child: strict, sporadic, lax, and none. Research reveals that the most damaging form is sporadic discipline. In this form the child seldom knows when he or she is right or wrong. Substance-abusing parents tend to administer this type of discipline. They are out of any parental loop most of the time; however, they randomly will appear with some form of discipline that is often not connected to their child's "bad behavior." Children subjected to this type of discipline tend to develop a dim view of justice in their life and the justice that exists in the larger society. The results of this pattern of sporadic discipline feed into the sociopathic viewpoint of distrust of others and a gangster lifestyle.

The children of substance abusers are also influenced by their parents' lifestyle to accept drug use as a way of resolving their emotional pain. Following in the path of their parents' substance abuse becomes for the gangster a way of ameliorating their painful feelings of low self-esteem and their sense of hopelessness in life.

Chris Britt. Reprinted by permission of Copley News Service.

In my work with delinquents, especially in psychiatric facilities, I have observed the impact created by drug-abusing parents on hundreds of youths who develop sociopathic personalities and become gangsters.

How One Boy Became a Gangster

One typical example is a thirteen-year-old wannabe (WB) whose gang name was L.K., short for "Little Killer." L.K. was emotionally and physically abused from the age of four, several times a week, by his drug addict father. The physical beatings and verbal abuse administered by his father often had little relationship to L.K.'s good or bad behavior. He would be beaten or verbally abused for a variety of "offenses" chosen at random by his irrational father. His father assaulted whenever he had a need to act out his drug-induced personal frustrations with the world around him; a convenient target was his son and his wife. According to L.K.,

> He would beat the shit out of me for no reason—just because he was loaded and mad at the world. I've always felt like a

punching bag, or maybe more like a piece of shit. If my own father thinks I'm a punk and a loser, maybe that's what I am.

The irrational behavior of L.K.'s father led to several consequences. The indiscriminate physical and verbal abuse had the effect of producing low self-esteem in the youth. He tended to feel humiliated and worthless. As a result of these feelings, he thought he was a loser. The only place where he found he had power, respect, and a reasonable sense of self was with his homies in the Venice gang Insane Baby Crips. The gang gave L.K. some level of the positive approval he so desperately needed and sought.

L.K.'s typical dysfunctional family helped to create a sociopathic gangster in several ways. First, the youth had no one in his family he felt he could trust. Second, there were no significant people in L.K.'s basic socialization who were positive role models, demonstrating how a person shows love and compassion to another person. A child can't learn to be compassionate if he never sees any examples of caring in his crucial early years. Third, because he was abused by his father, L.K. developed a low self-concept. In a reaction to these feelings of inadequacy, he developed a macho-syndrome that he acted out in the gang as a "little killer." Fourth, the gang gave this emotionally needy youth some sense of self-respect and power in his chaotic world. All of these socialization factors converged to produce a violent sociopathic gangster.

"By high school, I was ripe for anything that would give me that feeling of power. And that turned out to be [the Deceptinette gang]."

A Need for Power and Respect Encourages Gang Behavior

Isis Sapp-Grant, as told to Rosemarie Robotham

In the following viewpoint, Isis Sapp-Grant recounts her life as a member of one of New York City's most notorious female gangs, the Deceptinettes. She explains that she became involved in gang life because it gave her a sense of power and people feared and respected her. Sapp-Grant felt that the gang members were her true family and that no one else cared about her. She describes how she eventually turned her life around and left the gang with the help of supportive adults. Sapp-Grant is a social worker who does one-on-one therapy with children who are at risk of joining gangs. Rosemarie Robotham, who cowrote the article, is a writer for *Esquire*.

As you read, consider the following questions:
1. When did Sapp-Grant commit her first robbery?
2. According to the authors, why were the Deceptinettes unable to stop the violence?
3. What event ultimately led to Sapp-Grant leaving the Deceptinettes?

Excerpted from "Gang Girl: The Transformation of Isis Sapp-Grant," by Isis Sapp-Grant, as told to Rosemarie Robotham, *Essence*, August 1998. Reprinted with permission.

I didn't set out to join, let alone start, one of the most fearsome girl gangs in the city. But there I was. Me and my girls, the Deceptinettes, sisters of the male Decepticons—Decepts for short. The name was inspired by a silly Saturday morning cartoon, *Transformers*, which pitted the Decepticons, who were the bad guys, against the Autobots, who were the law enforcers.

This was 1986, and I was 15 years old, living in Brooklyn with my mother, who was a social worker, and my three sisters, who at the time were 18, 14 and 2. My lamer [father] wasn't around much; he and my mother were divorced. I'd just started at the High School of Graphic Communication Arts in Manhattan. My sisters were at different schools and, fortunately, they never got pulled into gangs. My personality was just different from theirs. I was more of a scrapper, always challenging my mother. As a kid, I thought I knew everything; I felt so powerful inside, and I couldn't understand why my mother didn't see that. She'd say, "Isis, why you always trying to act bigger than you are?" I craved recognition. So by high school, I was ripe for anything that would give me that feeling of power. And that turned out to be Decept.

Fighting for Respect

The Decepticon gang started in the early 1980's at Brooklyn Tech, one of the top high schools in New York City. The male gang leader, Derek, aka Megatron, became my boyfriend at one point. He was an honor student before he eventually got shot in the head and became paralyzed. Like Derek, when I first got into Decept, I didn't have a clue I'd be in for that kind of violence. I was mostly thinking about protecting myself.

I realized quickly that there were a lot of violent kids at school. But if I acted crazy, they kept their distance. And I found that the crazier I acted, the more respect I got. Some of the other girls who were new to the school noticed it, too, and started hanging with me. We weren't really a gang. Just friends. But we let it be known that if you messed with us, we would fight back. And that's how it started. There were about ten of us in the beginning, but soon more girls joined us, and other kids in the school began giving us money to protect them. A lot of us lived in Brooklyn and knew some of the Decepticons. They would back us up in fights sometimes. After a while, we decided to officially join forces with the guys and call ourselves the Deceptinettes.

Our ranks grew to about 70 over the next three years—that's how long I stayed in the gang. In all, there were several hundred Decept members, mostly male, at high schools throughout the city. We called our main headquarters—Derek's school—Cybertron, like in the cartoon, and our favorite gathering place was this park we called Signs of the Times. We even had a hand signal that we copied from the cartoon. In the beginning, Decept meetings were just a group of mostly Black and Hispanic teenagers hanging with their friends. The only problem was, to get respect on the street, we had to act like badasses. And things just escalated from there.

The First Robbery

The first time I ever robbed someone was on Halloween, a couple of months after I started high school. On this particular day, 50 or more Decepts decided to cut class and congregate in the park. And everybody was drinking Cisco and getting restless and mean. The next thing I remember, we went down into the nearby subway station and started racing up and down the platform and through the trains, robbing people, grabbing their stuff, beating them up if they resisted. I did it, too. I felt no boundaries, just this mad adrenaline rush. And at the time, I really liked the feeling that no one could mess with me. That I was invincible. Anything I wanted was mine.

I went home that evening with rings and gold chains and Louis Vuitton bags, and my mother didn't even notice. I knew she was having her own problems. I think she was depressed. Even though she had been a good mother to me and my sisters till then, she wasn't really paying attention to what I was getting into. And my sisters took their cue from her and left me alone.

That night I spread on my bed all the stuff I had stolen, and I was just amazed. I thought, That was too easy. After that, the violence really kicked in. And once it started, we couldn't stop because people were looking to get revenge on us, so we had to keep fighting just to protect ourselves. Plus, I think we really wanted to hurt people—as terrible as that sounds. We would play this game called one-punch knock-out: We'd stand outside the subway station and choose somebody and try to knock them out with one punch. I was good at that. Or we would sit around outside the school—we hardly ever went inside for classes anymore—and come up with ways to just mess with folks. By then, our rep had gotten so far out there that most people just gave us whatever we wanted. It was at the point where we could close down any school by calling the school office and telling them Decepts were coming. People were that scared.

Constant Violence

But they needed to be scared. We would get high on the violence. People were getting killed over the most stupid s---. I remember the first time I saw somebody die. We had beat up this boy's sister, and that night we were partying at some club. People were high out of their minds, and here comes this boy talking about "Leave my sister alone." This Jamaican guy I had a crush on—Frankie—he's like, "Just go away, man. You don't know what you're getting into. Just go." But the boy wouldn't leave, and some of the Decept girls started hitting him with baseball bats and hammers. Then the guys came outside and jumped into it, and one minute I saw the boy, the next minute I couldn't. They were just totally stomping him! Some guys fired shots, and all I remember was seeing the blood and thinking, This is all over hitting some stupid little girl.

I didn't know what to feel that night. I ran—we all ran—and found my way home in a blur. After a time, though, it didn't even matter. When you're in a gang, you see so much blood that you don't even care. It's almost like being a nurse. I would come home with blood on my shoes, blood on my coat, and my mother would say, "Where'd you get that coat?" And I'd say, "My friend gave it to me." Always some excuse. Then I'd go wash the blood off, wash my cuts and bruises—I never did get shot, thank God, and I'd think, Damn, she doesn't even see what's going on.

The way I felt was, no one cared about me and so I wasn't going to care about them. That's why I could watch somebody cry, plead, bleed, and it wouldn't touch me. It was as if we were all on a giant totem pole, and Black people were at the very bottom, and I was totally invisible. When you feel as invisible as I felt, you can become the most dangerous person in the world because you don't even care about your own life. I knew I wasn't going to live past 18. The only thing that gave me any pride was the fact that I was in Decept. . . .

Becoming Disillusioned with Gang Life

All that fighting and stealing eventually got me arrested, of course. When I turned 16, I was picked up for robbing some girl on the subway. I remember being handcuffed and taken to jail by these two Black undercover cops who must have been the most gorgeous men I had ever seen in my life. And I was so embarrassed. The handcuffs were like chains around my wrists. I felt like a slave. In my head, I kept saying, This is not you. You are not really like this. But then this other thought kept coming: Don't fool yourself, Isis. This is you.

I was in jail for a week and a half. I called my mother from the precinct house. She said, "Little girl, these people you're running with, they are not your friends. You have no friends. Your only friends are your family." But I still didn't get it. I thought Decept was my family. I loved my Decept sisters and brothers. We would do things that families did, like go to the beach and have picnics, baby showers and dance parties.

But we also went to funerals together. Members of Decept were dying all the time. Others of us were drug addicts, still others were in jail with life sentences, and some girls had had two, three babies with no-account guys. I was getting tired of losing everybody one by one, and, beneath all the toughness, I was hurting.

Finding the Will to Live

By age 17, I was going to funerals every week. And then Frankie got shot. He was my heart. Walking home after his funeral, I told myself, This does not matter. But that night I went into my mother's room and climbed into her bed. I needed to reach out in the dark and know she was there.

The whole night I dreamed about Frankie. The next morning I thought I was still dreaming because my mother was standing over me, and I had the weird sensation that she was looking down at me in my casket. She was crying. She said, "Isis, I want you to live. I want you to choose to live. I don't want to bury you ten feet under. I want to see your children."

From that day, things began to change. I started showing up for more classes so I wouldn't get into trouble. But sometimes I'd just want to be with my friends, and stuff would start happening. If I said, "I'm going home," they'd be like, "Isis, you're selling us out."

Seeking Love and a Family

Sometimes the love that teenagers get from gangs is greater than the love that they receive from their own families.

"We're like a family. We do sh-t together, we get money together. I'm going to bang for my dogs and they are going to bang for me," said Gerard.

But I wasn't satisfied with just one opinion. So I went to Joseph and asked him if he considered the Latin Kings to be like a family. He said, "Well, they are not like my family, they are my family."

Taz said if she joined the Bloods, she would "get the satisfaction of having another family."

With these three quotes, I put three and three together. Joseph, Gerard and Taz are all in the foster care system and they are all in gangs. Are these teens trying to recover a missing part of family that was lost a long time ago? Are they creating their own family because they honestly don't have a family? I came to the conclusion that a lot of kids think that the only way they will ever have a real family is to join a gang.

Anonymous, *Foster Care Youth United*, November/December 1998.

When I did go to class, a couple of my teachers began taking an interest. One was my writing teacher, a Black man named Mr. Mason. He encouraged me to write about what I was going through in the gang. The other one was Mrs. Beasley, a tough little seventysomething Black woman. Most teachers at my high school were scared to death of me, but not Mrs. Beasley. She would challenge me to try harder.

One other person helped save my life: a cop! The first time John Galea saw me, the cops had pulled me in for a lineup; he cussed me out, called me a little hoodlum. But he saw something else in me too, because he kept telling me, "Isis, you're smart. You can do better."

So these three people hooked up with my mother and the principal of the school, and they came up with a plan. They told me that if I would go to class and keep out of trouble, they would allow me to graduate. They arranged for me to attend Fisk University, the well-known Black school in Nashville. We knew I had to get out of New York because all these people who knew I didn't have Decept protection anymore were calling my house every day, threatening my family. As long as I was there, my mother and sisters weren't safe. Well, I graduated. I went to Fisk and cooled my heels for a year. But I just didn't fit in. People in Nashville still saw me as this badass New York City gang girl. I wasn't that person anymore. My consciousness had changed.

So after a year I transferred to the State University of New York at Stony Brook, Long Island. I met my husband-to-be, Alphonzo Grant, there, a big football-playing, clean-living jock who is now a lawyer. He was so sweet to me, even after I told him my history. I think he fell in love with me because by then I had started to fall in love with myself. I was taking good care of myself, studying hard, majoring in social work. And I meditated and prayed a lot. I was beginning to understand that God had a plan for me. After college, I got married and later went on to earn a master's degree in social work at New York University. Life can be amazing.

"Peer pressure is one of the most influential predicaments a youth might encounter."

Peer Pressure Influences Gang Behavior

Dale Greer

Peer pressure causes teens to make decisions they later regret, such as joining gangs, Dale Greer maintains in the following viewpoint. He cites the experiences of a boy named Hubert, whose inability to resist peer pressure led to his involvement with a gang that encouraged him to commit crimes such as carjacking, selling drugs, and stealing. Greer concludes by asserting that father figures are necessary to help instill the values teens need to resist peer pressure. Greer is an inmate at the Minnesota Correction Facility in Stillwater.

As you read, consider the following questions:

1. According to the author, what was Hubert's biggest burden?
2. How could Hubert's dilemma have improved, according to Greer?
3. According to Greer, why was Hubert's life condemned at age sixteen?

Reprinted from "The Devastation of Peer Pressure," by Dale Greer, *The Prison Mirror*, May 1998, by permission of *The Prison Mirror*, a publication of the Minnesota Correctional Facility in Stillwater, Minnesota.

Hubert Morris, a thirteen-year-old male, was raised in the housing projects in the inner city of North Minneapolis. His mother, a single parent of three siblings and also a welfare recipient, did her best to instill in her children moral values and self-discipline.

Hubert, his sister Pam, and brother Charles all attended church regularly because of Ms. Morris's religious background. They were obedient children. Had it not been for their worn-out garments, one wouldn't have guessed the Morris family resided in a low-income environment which was infested with dysfunctional activities such as drugs and gang affiliation.

Hubert Enters Gang Life

Although Hubert's school attendance was excellent and his aptitude was exceptionally progressive, he could not escape the reality of poverty. In fact, he was confronted with it everyday. The way the more fortunate kids teased him about his last year's clothing was beginning to irk him beyond his tolerance.

What young Hubert was experiencing was peer pressure. Peer pressure is one of the most influential predicaments a youth might encounter. Regardless of how unique his or her attributes are, once this element has taken its toll it could be detrimental to their education and future. It can represent acceptance as well as rejection.

In Hubert's case, his family financial situation was his biggest burden. Because his lack of material assets was so embarrassing, it drove him to cutting school. One thing led to another. It wasn't long before Hubert was committing crimes to provide for himself what his mother's income could not afford. He was committing offenses like shoplifting from department stores and stealing audio equipment out of vehicles.

His absence from school had begun to affect his grades, which added to his initial problems. Not only did he become a victim to peer pressure, but he'd flunked the eighth grade as well. The most important lesson Hubert failed to understand was that running away from a problem isn't the solution.

An Addiction to Pleasing People

Because Hubert was young and naive, he had no way of knowing that he'd subjected himself to being a people pleaser; an addiction that is as addictive and controlling as any mood-altering chemical or alcohol. To maintain his new reputation, Hubert became a cinch for his so-called friends to manipulate. What had initiated from minor meddling had gradually elevated to major trials and tribulations.

Hubert joined a clique of teenagers that was involved in everything from distributing drugs to carjacking. He was making more trouble for himself than he'd anticipated. On a couple of occasions, Ms. Morris received phone calls that related messages for her to pick Hubert up at juvenile detention. These particular arrests were pertaining to Hubert being inside of disorderly houses where crack was known to be sold.

As these events were transpiring, Hubert was falling further behind in school. He was now fifteen, with the eighth grade being his last grade completed. Running away from his primary situation had developed a severe barrier for him. From being too ashamed of falling so far behind, Hubert quit school altogether without attempting to make his grades up.

Over a period of two years, Hubert had converted from being obedient to a radical. That's just how devastating peer pressure can be if one does not stay focused on principles. It had Hubert going against his mother's good standards.

Facing the Court System

On his way to church he would detour to his friend's house, where he indulged in smoking marijuana. Since Hubert was the oldest of three children, it was easy for him to bribe his brother and sister with money so they wouldn't inform their mother of his behavior.

This went on until the Pastor phoned Ms. Morris to inquire about Hubert's ailment. When the Pastor had questioned Pam and Charles of Hubert's lack of church attendance, Pam the second oldest child said, "Hubert has been very sick lately."

Once Ms. Morris had gotten wise to her children's conniving demeanor, she made them go straight to their rooms after school for one month. But not Hubert. Believing that he was above punishment, he ran away from home. A month later, he was apprehended and detained in detention. The court system had seen enough of Hubert's misconduct. The judge ordered him to enter a residential group home for problematic teenage boys. Hubert was to remain there until he improved in school and changed his attitude.

Two weeks hadn't passed before Hubert's so-called friends learned of his whereabouts and forced him into absconding the program. Hubert was corrigible, but like so many other teenagers who wanted to be accepted by their fellow peers, he had easily gotten himself caught up with a group that wasn't so simple to get rid of. What had been his choice from the beginning had turned into obligation by force.

Peer Pressure as a Risk Factor

This table summarizes risk factors for youth gang membership that have been identified in studies using many types of research methods.

Risk Factors:

- High commitment to delinquent peers
- Low commitment to positive peers
- Street socialization
- Gang members in class
- Friends who use drugs or who are gang members
- Friends who are drug distributors
- Interaction with delinquent peers

James C. Howell, *Youth Gangs: An Overview*, 1998.

Hubert's dilemma could have made a turn for the better had he put more faith in the staff at the group home and the local authorities. Instead, he allowed himself to be influenced and petrified by the peer pressure.

A Ruined Life

He stayed on the run one year before he was finally captured again. Only this time, he was facing an additional offense. Hubert had graduated to the big league; he'd been indicted on murder charges. Even though he wasn't the perpetrator who actually committed the offense, he became an accessory because of his affiliation with the group that was responsible for the malevolent deed.

Now at age sixteen Hubert's life was condemned before he was able to make a life for himself, all because of his urgent desire to be equal from a material perspective. Little did he know about authentic values, for material is only temporary; here today, gone tomorrow.

As Hubert lay in his double bunk cell awaiting his sentencing date, he said to his cellmate, "Had I known what I know now, I wouldn't have ever joined 'The Posse.' After all I've done to prove my loyalty to them, not one of the members who remain at large came to my aid."

It's common for kids that are products of broken homes to make a wrong decision, such as the one Hubert made. In certain instances, a teenager needs more than just a mother to ensure his success. Having a father figure around to instill in him good traits of being a man, a male youth is more apt to fend off the peer pressure that he might undergo. To all who it may concern, *don't be a victim of peer pressure!*

> "[Eric] Wright's life and death supported the negative messages of gangster rap—to live life fast and hard before dying."

Gangster Rap Glorifies Violent Behavior

Rick Landre, Mike Miller, and Dee Porter

Gangster rap often glamorizes the gang lifestyle, Rick Landre, Mike Miller, and Dee Porter claim in the following viewpoint. They cite the experiences of famous rappers whose brief lives and popular careers were marked by arrests and controversy as proof that the gangster image can influence gang violence. However, the authors note, this influence is not limited to gangster rap; white racist bands can have a similar impact. Rick Landre, Mike Miller, and Dee Porter are the authors of *Gangs: A Handbook for Community Awareness*, from which this viewpoint is excerpted.

As you read, consider the following questions
1. What is the tragedy of gangster rap's popularity, in the authors' view?
2. What do the authors believe was the likeliest cause of Tupac Shakur and Christopher Wallace's murders?
3. Why do the authors question the intentions of the producers of the *Bangin' on Wax* album?

Excerpted from *Gangs: A Handbook for Community Awareness*, by Rick Landre, Mike Miller, and Dee Porter. Copyright ©1997 by Rick Landre, Mike Miller, and Dee Porter. Reprinted by permission of Facts On File, Inc.

The music most often associated with street gangs is a form of hip-hop music commonly known as *gangster rap* or *gangsta rap*. The origin of rap can be traced to the east coast of the United States in the late 1970s. Artists appeared on street corners, in underground clubs, and anywhere else an appreciative audience could be found. Commercial recordings of rap artists were few and far between until 1979, when the Sugarhill Gang released an album called Rapper's Delight, marking the commercial emergence of rap.

Gangster Rap Is Popular

Throughout the 1980s rap became more popular, moving quickly across the country. Groups using mild lyrics and themes gave way to groups whose hard angry raps were laced with profanity. The trend continued through the early nineties with few restrictions on the vulgarity of rap lyrics. As the image of the gangster rapper became more closely tied to rap, rap lyrics talked more about life in the inner city and the social conscience, or lack thereof, of the artist.

Despite gangster rap's popularity among youth, radio stations across the country have called the music "socially irresponsible" and have edited offending lyrics, limited play, or refused to play it at all. Such actions were the subject of many feature news stories in 1993. Protests by several groups against gangster rap's derogatory portrayal of women and blacks became national news. Despite these objections, the saga of gangster rap continues. The tragedy of this situation is the failure of rap artists and recording companies to responsibly address the influence that their music has on young listeners. In September 1995, as a public response to outcries about the negativity and violence espoused by gangster rap, Time Warner divested itself of Interscope Records, which distributed its rap artists' music.

Sales analysis indicates that gangster rap is popular among blacks, Asians, Hispanics, and whites. Fascination with the "gangsta" image is creating a cult following for the "gangsta rap" stars, who cultivate an image as drug dealing gangbangers because that is what their fans admire.

The death in March 1995 of rapper Easy-E, a former member of the early rap group NWA (Niggaz With Attitude), forged the connection between image and reality. Easy-E, whose real name was Eric Wright, was only 31 at the time of his death from AIDS. Wright was born and raised in Compton, California, a gang-infested area of the Los Angeles metropolitan area.

A former drug dealer, Wright was a member of a notorious Compton-based street gang and used his gang credentials to promote the authenticity of his music. Wright even bragged about having fathered seven children by six different women, part of his image as a ruthless womanizer.

By having lived the life he rapped about, Wright promoted an image as an authentic gangster rapper. He was not a "studio gangster," as fans have labeled many rappers. Wright and NWA had a big impact on rap culture with the release of their 1988 album, *Straight Outta Compton*. It depicted vividly the lifestyle of street gangs, with lyrics about drive-by shootings, drug dealing, and confrontations with police. Its depiction of violence helped to sell over 2 million copies of the album despite the lack of radio play due to graphic contents.

Wright's life and death supported the negative messages of gangster rap—to live life fast and hard before dying. By dying young, Wright's immortalization as a rap star was ensured among young hip-hop followers.

Art Copying Life

Several other rap stars have also demonstrated that their art mirrors their life. Dr. Dre, another product of the Compton, California, gang scene, has a police record that helps to promote his gangster persona. He lives as though adhering to his own lyrics—"Rat-a-tat and a tat like that/Never hesitate to put a nigga on his back." Even after achieving celebrity as a rapper, Dr. Dre beat a woman in a Los Angeles night club.

The ongoing saga of Calvin Broadus, known more popularly as Snoop Doggy Dogg, is another example. He's been arrested for possession and sale of cocaine, charged with a weapons violation, and linked to the murder of a rival gang member by his bodyguard. Broadus followers believe these incidents help legitimize his work. The incidents do not seem to have hurt the sales of his 1993 release *Doggy Style* and the 1994 album *Murder Was the Case*. Despite this popularity, Snoop Doggy Dogg said, "As far as my acting career, I want a role of an attorney. I don't want to be remembered as a gang member."

Tupac Shakur, another successful actor and rapper, is also known for his scrapes with the law. In 1993, he was arrested for allegedly being involved in the shooting of two Atlanta, Georgia, police officers. Within three weeks, while he was out on bail, he was again charged as an accomplice, along with two associates, to the forcible sodomy and sexual abuse of a woman in a New York City hotel, a crime for which he received a sentence of four and a half years. Although he was imprisoned at the time and unable to promote or make a video, Shakur's latest album release, *Me Against the World*, was *Billboard* magazine's number-one album for several weeks during March and April of 1995.

Shakur's short span of stardom came to a halt when he died on Friday the 13th of September 1996. Six days earlier Shakur was the victim of his image after being shot several times by unknown assailants while riding in the car of Marion "Suge" Knight, the president of Death Row Records. This undoubtedly would raise his gangster image to an even higher level of reality and sell more albums.

Another rap artist, Christopher Wallace, known as the Notorious B.I.G., a.k.a. Biggie Smalls, was gunned down in March 1997 by unknown assailants. Wallace was known as an East Coast–style rap artist in contrast to Tupac Shakur's West Coast style. Rumors began to fly about a feud between gangs on each coast of the United States being responsible for the deaths of both rappers. The truth, however, is probably that each was a victim of his own hyped image that he created for himself, and it just got out of control. Gangsta rap may have reached its peak as record sales have begun to slow for the genre. Even Dr. Dre has softened his image and is said to be going back to a rhythm-and-blues style of music.

Exploiting Rap's Popularity

Music recording companies have not been shy in attempting to exploit gang rivalries and interest in gang lifestyle. In

1993, Dangerous Records released an album titled *Bangin'*
on Wax. Sixteen supposed members of various Blood and
CRIP gangs from the Los Angeles area who were amateur
rappers were featured on the album. To enhance the mystic
image of the rappers, their faces were covered by bandannas
in the appropriate blue or red colors, and they were listed on
the album only by their street monikers. The album's producers claim their intent was to bring rival groups together
to show them their similarities. Such peaceful intentions,
however, were not evidenced in the album's selections, with
such titles as "I Killed Ya Dead Homies" and "Another Slob
Bites the Dust." The album producers also attempted to
claim community responsibility by donating a percentage of
the album's profits to recreational facilities in Compton and
South Central Los Angeles.

Denied a True Culture

Definitions of manhood and womanhood (more specific
identities) are derived from culture. If, as in the African
American community, you have people who have been de-
nied their culture by White supremacism, and youth who believe they have no culture, the African American community
will devise one for themselves. Therefore, you will have a
"hip-hop" culture full of youth with definitions of their identity and the rites of passage into manhood/womanhood defined by Euro-American guns, drug retailing, foreign-made
gym shoes, White distributed music, 40s, sexism, and misguided pronouncements of righteousness. Moreover, you
will have the glamorization of the killing of other African
Americans. Youth will know Tupac Shakur and glamorize or
rationalize his self-destructive "thug life" but remain ignorant of Mutulu and Afeni Shakur.

Errol A. Henderson, *Journal of Black Studies*, January 1996.

Music, as an influence on gang violence and image, is not
limited to the black rap artists who have received the most
media and public attention. Several bands popular with
Skinheads and white racist groups do not get equivalent
coverage and are therefore largely unknown to most people.
The groups' albums are not carried by most music stores as
a result of their limited appeal. Some such music is only

available through bootleg tapes passed around at meetings of white hate groups. These groups, including Screwdriver and White Rider, may appear to the uninformed as two more malevolent heavy metal rock groups, but careful listening reveals lyrics as vulgar, racist, and violent as those of the gangster rappers.

Periodical Bibliography

The following articles have been selected to supplement the diverse views presented in this chapter. Addresses are provided for periodicals not indexed in the *Readers' Guide to Periodical Literature*, the *Alternative Press Index*, the *Social Sciences Index*, or the *Index to Legal Periodicals and Books*.

Richard L. Dukes, Ruben O. Martinez, and Judith A. Stein
"Precursors and Consequences of Membership in Youth Gangs," *Youth and Society*, December 1997. Available from Sage Publications, 2455 Teller Rd., Thousand Oaks, CA 91320.

Joseph L. Galloway and Bruce Selcraig
"Into the Heart of Darkness," *U.S. News & World Report*, March 8, 1999.

Nina George Hacker
"Gangs: When Families Fail," *Family Voice*, February 1997. Available from Concerned Women for America, 370 L'Enfant Promenade SW, Suite 800, Washington, DC 20024.

Errol A. Henderson
"Black Nationalism and Rap Music," *Journal of Black Studies*, January 1996. Available from Sage Publications, 2455 Teller Rd., Thousand Oaks, CA 91320.

Arturo Hernandez, interviewed by *Children's Voice*
"Voices for Children: Arturo Hernandez," *Children's Voice*, Spring 1998. Available from Child Welfare League of America, 440 First St. NW, Third Floor, Washington, DC 20001-2085.

Ann Hulbert
"The Influence of Anxiety," *New Republic*, December 7, 1998.

Juvenile Justice Bulletin
"Program of Research on the Causes and Correlates of Delinquency," October 1998. Available from Juvenile Justice Clearinghouse, PO Box 6000, Rockville, MD 20849-6000.

Juvenile Justice Update
"Who Joins Gangs and Why? Seattle Study Sheds Light on the Problem," August/September 1997. Available from 4490 U.S. Route 27, PO Box 585, Kingston, NJ 08528.

Toni Locy
"Like Mother, Like Daughter," *U.S. News & World Report*, October 4, 1999.

Peter L. Patton
"The Gangstas in Our Midst," *Urban Review*, March 1998. Available from Human Sciences Press, 233 Spring St., New York, NY 10013-1578.

Lening Zhang, John W. Welte, and William F. Wieczorek
"Youth Gangs, Drug Use, and Delinquency," *Journal of Criminal Justice*, March/April 1999. Available from Elsevier Science, 655 Avenue of the Americas, New York, NY 10010-5107.

How Widespread Is the Problem of Gangs?

Chapter Preface

Gangs are not restricted to Los Angeles, Chicago, or New York. A 1996 survey by the Office of Juvenile Justice and Delinquency Prevention revealed that 57 percent of suburban counties and 25 percent of rural counties reported a gang presence. Consequently, violent gangs are appearing in unlikely areas, such as Utah, where youths reportedly involved in the Straight Edge movement have been blamed for murder and other violence.

The Straight Edge movement began in the early 1980s as an offshoot of the punk scene. Followers eschew alcohol, drugs, smoking, promiscuous sex, and often meat. While most Straight Edgers are not violent, some are less tolerant toward those who do not follow the same lifestyle. It is the more violent adherents that many people charge have been causing gang problems in Utah.

According to an article by Louis Sahagun in the *Los Angeles Times*, more than one thousand violent Straight Edgers live in Utah. Among the violence that has been reportedly committed by them is the stabbing death of a fifteen-year-old Salt Lake City youth and the bombings of a fur farm in 1997. Brad Harmon, a deputy in the Salt Lake County Sheriff's Department, has labeled these Straight Edgers "suburban terrorists."

However, while these bombings and assaults have garnered much attention, some people argue that the threat of Straight Edgers has been overstated. According to Steve Lopez, writing for *Time*, Straight Edgers committed only three of the two hundred gang-related felonies in Salt Lake City in 1998. Many Straight Edgers also disavow these gangs' reported connections to the movement. In an interview with the webzine *Pastepunk*, Greg Bennick, the lead singer of the hardcore punk band Trial, contends: "There are no straight edge gangs in Utah . . . what happened in Utah is the unfortunate and misguided connection of straight edge adherents with animal rights activists."

As gangs expand beyond major urban areas, the potential problems they represent spread along with them. In the following chapter, the authors evaluate the extent of the gang problem.

> *"Crime surveys and statistics suggest that gangs are posing a more serious crime problem than in the past."*

Gangs Present a Serious Threat

Steven R. Wiley

In the following viewpoint, Steven R. Wiley asserts that gangs present an increasingly serious crime problem. According to Wiley, gangs have become more involved in drug trafficking, while the most visible gang crime is murder. Wiley also asserts that the number and type of gangs are growing and that Indian and ethnic gangs pose a growing threat. Wiley is the chief of the violent crimes and major offenders section for the Federal Bureau of Investigation.

As you read, consider the following questions:
1. In the author's view, what are two basic obstacles to addressing gang activity?
2. What are some of the gangs that have particularly well-organized drug operations, as listed by Wiley?
3. According to the National Drug Intelligence Center survey cited by Wiley, what percentage of the 301 jurisdictions that responded to the survey reported gang activity?

Excerpted from Steven R. Wiley's testimony before the U.S. Senate Committee on the Judiciary, April 23, 1997.

Two of the basic obstacles in addressing gang activity in communities around the nation are the absence of a universal definition for gangs, and the difficulty in documenting the nature and extent of gang-related criminal activity. While some communities acknowledge difficulties in dealing with the problem, they fail to concede that they have a gang problem until the gangs become firmly entrenched.

Defining Gangs

The Federal Bureau of Investigation defines a Violent Street Gang/Drug Enterprise as a criminal enterprise having an organizational structure, acting as a continuing criminal conspiracy, which employs violence and any other criminal activity to sustain the enterprise.

The term street gang is the term preferred by key local law enforcement agencies because it includes juveniles and adults, and designates the location of gangs and most of its criminal behavior. A street gang is a group of people that form an allegiance based on various social needs and engage in acts injurious to public health and safety. Members of street gangs engage in (or have engaged in) gang-focused criminal activity either individually or collectively, they create an atmosphere of fear and intimidation within the community.

Street gangs have been documented in cities in the United States throughout most of the country's history, but crime surveys and statistics suggest that gangs are posing a more serious crime problem than in the past. In some cities, such as Chicago, Illinois, and Los Angeles, California, gangs are credited with an alarming share of violent crime, especially homicides. And while reports conflict about the extent to which gangs play an organized role in drug trafficking, the vast majority of gang cases investigated by the FBI revealed that drug trafficking was the primary criminal enterprise that supported the gang, [but] was not necessarily the sole purpose for the gang's existence.

Gangs and the Drug Trade

Gangs have been involved with the lower levels of the drug trade for many years, but their participation skyrocketed with the arrival of "crack" cocaine. Almost overnight, a major industry was born, with outlets in every neighborhood, tens of thousands of potential new customers and thousands of sales jobs available. In slightly over a decade, street gangs have become highly involved in drug trafficking at all levels. Intelligence developed through investigations has revealed extensive interaction among individuals belonging to gangs across the Nation. This interaction does not take the conceptual form of traditional organized crime. It is more a loose network of contacts and associations that come together as needed to support individual business ventures.

There are, however, some street gangs that possess structured organization in their drug operations. In cities such as Chicago and New Haven, the Black Gangster Disciple Nation, Vice Lords, and Latin Kings have a more recognized organizational structure, funneling profits upward through the organization.

Street gang-related violence and drug activity, however, are not necessarily synonymous. While street gangs may specialize in entrepreneurial activities like drug dealing, their gang-related lethal violence is more likely to grow out of turf conflicts than from the entrepreneurial activity. Drug markets indirectly influence violence by bringing rival gang members into proximity with one another, as most street gang violence involves inter-gang conflicts.

The Extent of Gang Crimes

By far the most visible and frightening of gang crimes is murder. Contrary to popular belief, most murders committed by gang members are not random shootings nor are they direct disputes over drugs or some other crime. While those types of gang homicides do occur, most are the product of old-fashioned fights over turf, status and revenge. Drive-by shootings and other confrontations of this kind typically involve small sets of gang members acting more or less on their own, not large groups representing an entire gang. But each attack creates a chain reaction of complicity, vengeance and commitment.

A study conducted by the Illinois Criminal Justice Information Authority focused on intra-gang, inter-gang and non-gang member victimization. The study examined 956 street gang-related homicides which occurred in Chicago, Illinois, between 1987 and 1994. Of the 956 street gang-related homicides, 10.8 percent were determined to be intragang murders, 74.8 percent were intergang murders, and 14.4 percent were murders of non-gang victims by a gang member. Gang members, male and female alike, commit crimes in numbers far out of proportion to their share of the general population. Consistently, more than half of all gang members tend to be repeat offenders.

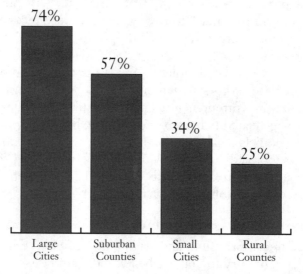

Percentage of Jurisdictions Reporting Gangs in 1996, by Area Type

74% — Large Cities
57% — Suburban Counties
34% — Small Cities
25% — Rural Counties

Office of Juvenile Justice and Delinquency Prevention, *1996 National Youth Gang Survey*, July 1999.

In the latter part of the 1980's this country was impacted by the migration of inner-city gang members across America. This migration from metropolitan areas such as Los Angeles and Chicago set in motion a social phenomenon of violence and anti-authority defiance among youth. Fueled primarily by family relocation rather than a desire to expand into new criminal markets, the migration drastically altered the violent crime problem of communities across the Nation.

The National Drug Intelligence Center, commonly known

as NDIC, completed a National Street Gang Report in June 1996. The study was conducted by NDIC's Violent Crimes/ Gang Program in an attempt to evaluate the relationship between drugs and gang-related activity and the violent crime that results when these two factors are present. The study is also a useful tool to gauge the level at which nationally recognized street gangs have successfully established footholds in communities where heretofore, gang activity was nonexistent. In order to obtain a foundation of information regarding gang activity from a national perspective, NDIC surveyed municipal and county law enforcement agencies throughout the United States.

Gangs Are Everywhere

Based upon a review of the survey responses received from 301 law enforcement agencies throughout the United States, NDIC noted the following trends:

- Gang activity was reported in 88 percent of the 301 jurisdictions responding to the survey and in 98 percent of the 120 jurisdictions with populations over 100,000.
- Gang activity is not confined to major metropolitan areas and was reported in 68 percent of the 59 responding jurisdictions with populations under 25,000 and in 78 percent of the 120 responding jurisdictions with populations under 50,000.
- Over 7,400 individual gang sets were identified.
- Chicago-based gangs, such as the Black Gangster Disciples, Vice Lords and Almighty Latin Kings were reported in 110 of the responding jurisdictions in 35 states.
- Gangs claiming affiliation with the Blood and/or Crip sets, such as the Rolling 60's Crips, Hoover Crips and Bounty Hunter Bloods, were reported in 180 responding jurisdictions in 42 states.
- Hispanic Gangs, such as Mara Salvatrucha, La Eme, and the 18th Street Gang, were reported in 167 jurisdictions in 41 states and made up 29 percent of all gangs reported.
- White gangs were reported in 157 jurisdictions in 44 states.
- Asian gangs were reported in 104 jurisdictions in 41 states.

It is important to note that when a gang has taken the name

of a nationally known gang, this does not necessarily indicate that the gang is part of a group with a national infrastructure. According to the NDIC Report the majority of gangs do not have interstate connections or a hierarchical structure. These loosely structured gangs are often more violent and criminally active than the gangs they seek to imitate. . . .

Violent street gangs have also become a significant problem in Indian Country. On the Navajo Reservation in Arizona alone there are approximately 55 street gangs, many of which have some affiliation with gangs in California, Phoenix, Albuquerque, and Chicago. These gangs have been responsible for a dramatic increase in violent crimes in the Navajo Nation. The Salt-River Pima-Maricopa Indian Community near Scottsdale, Arizona experienced a significant increase in murders and drive-by shootings between 1993 and 1994. Current trends indicate that Indian gangs are mirroring the gang activity occurring in the communities surrounding Indian Country. Some Indian gang members are claiming allegiance with the larger nationally known gang "nations," such as Folks.

Ethnic gang criminal activity has also been increasing during the last few years. Ethnic gangs possess many of the characteristics of the more organized street gangs. The distinction between the two is that ethnic gangs require, as a condition of membership, that their members belong to a particular race or ethnic group. Among ethnic gangs, Jamaican posses and Asian gangs are considered by many law enforcement officials to pose a growing threat.

New Efforts by Law Enforcement

The current increase in gang activity, including migration into previously gang-free communities, has required federal, state and local law enforcement agencies to adjust resources to deal with the resulting increase in violent crimes and drug trafficking. Until the early 1990s, these problems were deemed to lie largely outside the mandate of federal law enforcement. However, recent efforts and initiatives from federal law enforcement have had an impact in stemming the tide of gang-related crime that is destabilizing urban, suburban, and rural communities.

"Strict adherence to a broad definition obviously creates a gang, . . . where perhaps no gang exists at all!"

Inaccurate Definitions Exaggerate the Gang Threat

Francine Garcia-Hallcom

Overly broad definitions of "gangs" lead to an exaggeration of their threat, asserts Francine Garcia-Hallcom in the following viewpoint. She notes that many youth who do not belong to gangs have relatives or close friends who are gang members and therefore, they are likely to associate with gangs to some degree. She contends that this close association leads many cities and police departments to incorrectly identify youths as gang members, thus inflating the number of gangs and gangsters. Garcia-Hallcom is a professor at California State University at Northridge.

As you read, consider the following questions:
1. In the author's view, what do inaccurate gang definitions run the risk of initiating?
2. How can antisocial criminals prevent being labeled gang members, according to the author?
3. According to Garcia-Hallcom, why do police agencies sometimes exaggerate gang statistics?

Excerpted from "An Urban Ethnography of Latino Street Gangs in Los Angeles and Ventura Counties," by Francine Garcia-Hallcom, at www.csun.edu/~hcchs006/6.html. Reprinted by permission of the author.

On the surface, one may think that kids gone astray need to be rescued, not defined. Nonetheless, there are subtle differences between topologies: between being gang-involved and committing gang delinquency, between non-gang and gang delinquency, and between gang graffiti vandalism and tagger insignias. When these fine distinctions are overlooked, techniques aimed at lowering gang delinquency in and of themselves do not prove fruitful in lowering overall crime rates.

A Lack of Accurate Definitions

Even Frederic Thrasher's 1936 premiere study of gangs was criticized for lacking a "core definition." As a result, a host of youth group activities as diverse as fraternities to street corner gangs were analyzed in that now classic research work. Today, astute journalists, prosecutors, legislators, and scholars generally evade definitions, yet there is a tendency to be completely unfettered about using the words "gang member" and even applying them to individuals.

In the prominent sociologist Malcolm W. Klein's definition of gangs, perceived impressions were allowed, so that public surmising often determined a gang's traits. However, public perception, as it turns out, is more often than not unreliable, although in the current research same-age-peers seemed to know exactly who was and who was not gang-affiliated.

At any rate, definitions run the risk of initiating a wave of anti-gang hysteria and the ensuing array of ineffective and costly anti-gang activities: namely, curfews and sweeps—the unfortunate, but prevailing strategies currently used in many parts of the country.

Without some kind of working definition, another commonly occurring predicament soon surfaces. Generalizations are applied to white supremacy groups, bikers, Asian gangs, African American and Latino gangs alike when in reality there are clearly discernable differences among these groups.

Typical Definitions

Among social scientists in the academic world, definitions are most often determined in terms of variables, many of which are derived from social learning theory. Other studies use personal-biographical characteristics. And still others depend on observations and reports of various kinds like those used in the current research.

Like the city of San Diego's definition, most descriptions depict gangs as groups that have identifiable leadership, a geographic, economic or criminal turf, regular and continuous fellowship, engaging in criminal activity. San Diego's definition may be a bit too broad in that it does not require ethnic or social group membership and could, therefore, be applied to any criminal organization.

Police departments across the country have similar definitions. Some add that the individual to be defined as a "gang" member admits gang membership, has tattoos, wears gang clothing and paraphernalia associated with a specific gang, has a police record and engages in criminal activity. Thus, if a youth is arrested while in the company of a known gang member, the errant youngster is considered a gang member as well—and on record! Ironically, the truly antisocial criminal can altogether escape being labelled a gang member by working alone like [an] "independent operator."

Additionally, strict adherence to a broad definition obviously creates a gang, at least reportedly (and customarily creates with it the accompanying public panic) where perhaps no gang exists at all!

Some parts of the country call gangs ethnic, organized, and engaged in criminal activity—Kansas City Police Department for example. Kansas City's criteria also includes age range 13 to 24, and comments that the gang member is usually from a dysfunctional family (i.e., single parent or abusing parent).

And herein lies a topic for yet another investigation in and of itself: single parent homes are not always dysfunctional. Many two parent homes are! The loopholes in the various definitions are unwieldy.

Close Associations Do Not Always Indicate Gang Membership

The California Youth Gang Task Force drafted a definition of a youth gang to serve as the conceptual focus of its 1988 publication entitled "Guide for the Investigation and Prosecution of Youth Gang Violence in California." It established procedure for investigations of youth gang-related crimes—i.e., how to set up gang files, etc.—and to that end criteria are listed: (1) subject admits being a member of a gang. (2) Subject has tattoos, clothing, and gang paraphernalia. (3) Subject has close association with known gang members.

A Difficulty with Definitions

While some definitions of gang-related behavior do, in fact, properly use the term, much of what is labeled as gang-related behavior is really not gang related at all. Police may classify an incident as gang related simply because the individual involved is a gang member. Cheryl Maxson and Malcolm Klein refer to this as a member-based definition. Other departments may use a motive-based definition, whereby an incident is gang related because the individual gang member acts on the gang's behalf.

Experts on gangs also have great difficulty in reaching consensus on what constitutes a gang, partly because youth gangs and delinquent groups have characteristic differences. In the 1950s and 1960s, researchers viewed the delinquent gang and the delinquent group as identical. The tendency to consider youth gangs and delinquent groups as the same continues today, especially when juveniles are studied.

Bureau of Justice Assistance, *Addressing Community Gang Problems: A Practical Guide*, May 1998.

Many non-gang affiliated subjects admit having "close associations" with gang members, and in most cases non-gang affiliated youths have boyhood pals, cousins, uncles, and even brothers who are in gangs. Although the former distance themselves from the gangs, many non-gang affiliated youths are compelled to associate, at least to some extent, with gang members in order to keep the peace. Often they not only live on the same street, but in the same buildings! The rule of this jungle is to avoid trouble by saying "hello" and looking away quickly. To completely ignore someone can be misconstrued.

Another reason to seek out a formal definition for the word "gang," which does have some impact on striking a blow against their terrorizing the streets, concerns the accessibility of services available for marginally involved youths who might be salvaged. A very restrictive definition limits the numbers and subsequent funds available to a community. Thus, police agency statistics are sometimes a bit exaggerated in order to maximize the benefit to the community.

Relying on Suspects' Self-Identification

Defining who is and who is not a gang member is further complicated in many cases by suspects who lie to police. Certainly, a good many wannabes identify themselves as gang members for the prestige they gain among peers.

Clearly, other political considerations and complications taint available data. However, because no funds are being solicited in the current study—either to begin or sustain programs of any kind—this [viewpoint] . . . attempts to remain uncluttered by the usual political considerations.

Instead, the gang-affiliated are classified here according to their own testimony and seconded by that of their contemporaries as well as by that of non-gang affiliated peers from the same neighborhood. To a lesser extent this viewpoint also addresses some of the same characteristics delineated by other research scientists in other studies. After all, gang members do indeed have a number of qualities in common.

For example, Latino gang members are unquestionably groups from the same neighborhood as defined in other data; however, in a good many Latino barrios there are also ex-offenders from the same penal facility, but not necessarily the same neighborhood who are "adjunct members," for lack of a better term. These were all males in the current sample and were consistently referred to as "o.k. guys," "a good vato," "firme," "mi carnal," etc. These individuals are free to come in and out of the turf at will. They "hang-out" with the gang and are perceived as members although they may reside clear across town or even in another part of the state. The literature gives no mention of this type of member who may be "hard core" and participating fully with the gang members when he is in their turf.

"I think law enforcement . . . [tends] to underestimate the number of girls [in gangs]."

Girl Gangs Are a Growing Problem

Gini Sikes, interviewed by Lori Leibovich

The following viewpoint is an interview of Gini Sikes, author of 8 Ball Chicks: A Year in the Violent World of Girl Gangsters, *by Lori Leibovich, a writer for* Salon, *an online magazine. Sikes contends that girls are becoming increasingly involved in gangs. She asserts that law enforcement tends to underestimate the number of girl gang members because they do not believe women pose a criminal threat. Sikes argues that girl gangsters commit many of the same crimes as their male counterparts but notes that differences exist between female and male gangs.*

As you read, consider the following questions:

1. Why do girls join gangs, in Sikes' view?
2. According to Sikes, what is one major difference between girl gangsters and guy gangsters?
3. How can a girl leave a gang without becoming pregnant, according to Sikes?

Reprinted, with permission, from "Bangin' with the Girls," an interview of Gini Sikes by Lori Leibovich. This article first appeared in *Salon* (April 9, 1997), an online magazine, at www.salonmagazine.com. An online version remains in the *Salon* archives.

The faces of gangsters—on television, at the movies and in the obituary column—are almost always male. But [the] book, *8 Ball Chicks: A Year in the Violent World of Girl Gangsters*, examines the role of young women in urban gang culture. The book's author, Gini Sikes, spent two years on the streets of Los Angeles, Milwaukee and San Antonio chronicling the violent lives of dozens of young women.

Sikes' claim that the number of girl gangsters is rising is corroborated by Brian Riley of the Milwaukee Police Gang Crime Division. Her finding that girl gangs operate essentially as auxiliaries to male gangs is supported by detective Robert Borg of the San Antonio Police Department's Youth Crime Division. "Basically the girls are property," he said.

The Extent of Girl Gangs

Salon spoke with Gini Sikes about the world of girl gangs, what attracts—and repels—female gang wannabes, and how degrading the whole experience turns out to be.

Lori Leibovich: Why the title "8 Ball Chicks"?

Sikes: The name comes from a gang in San Antonio. One of the ways a female gang can form is through a ladies auxiliary. In San Antonio I met the Eight Ball posse, a boy gang, and eventually they introduced me to the Lady Eights which was the girl gang. The boys referred to them as the "8 ball chicks." I liked the name because of the expression "behind the 8 ball," meaning being in a tough position, which many of these girls are.

How many girl gang members are there in the U.S.?

It's hard to get good numbers. Justice Department figures say there are 650,000 gang members nationwide. The rule of thumb is that 10 to 15 percent of those are female.

So there could be as many as 100,000 girl gang members. Why don't we hear very much about them?

Traditionally, cops and social workers have ignored them because they believe women don't pose as much of a threat. I think law enforcement overestimates the numbers of young, minority males—based on such things as how they dress and where they hang out—whereas they tend to underestimate the number of girls.

For example, one night I was driving in South Central and

I was pulled over by the police and made to get on my knees because I was hanging out with boys who were wearing gang colors. I'm sure that had I been with girls in the same environment, wearing the same clothes in the same neighborhood, they would not have pulled me over.

The Daily Life of Girl Gangsters

While researching the book you practically lived with girl gangsters in three cities—San Antonio, Milwaukee and Los Angeles. What did they do all day?

Ninety percent of the time they did nothing. They would go to "ditching" parties where a group of kids would skip school and hang out. Their neighborhoods had little to offer—no recreation centers or youth programs. Often if the cops know you are affiliated with a certain gang they won't let you hang out in certain places, like parks. So there really is nowhere for these kids to go. And there are no midnight basketball programs for girl gangs.

Even if there were, do you think these girls would participate? Wouldn't that seem uncool?

I think they would participate. They need and want hands-on attention from adults.

We associate young male gangs with crime. Is it the same with girl gangs?

It's incremental. Girls join gangs to be accepted. Often girls that don't fit in can find a place in a gang. Gangs will accept fat girls and girls with acne—as long as they can fight well. Once a girl is in the gang it becomes very seductive because people are now scared of them and that gives the girl power. They start to "act out." This leads to criminal activity because you can't just hang out in a gang forever—you have to prove yourself. You have to fight or sleep with a bunch of guys in the gang.

Are the crimes the same?

The same as male gang bangers—assaults, robberies, carjackings, joy rides, drive-bys. The girls don't commit as many murders, but they do disfigure other girls with razors. If a girl has to stay home because she's pregnant or has a young child sometimes she will run drug rings.

You portray girl gangsters as just as violent and emotionally dis-

turbed as male gang bangers. What are some of the differences?

Girls tend to have a worse home life. Many of them came from homes where their father or stepfathers were molesting them. No one was listening to them so they would run out on the street and pound on the first person who triggered their temper.

One main difference between girls and guys is that with the girls there is a real acceptance of homosexuality. Homosexuality exists among male gangs, but it is not acknowledged. I knew some gay Latina gang members who looked indistinguishable from the guys down to their boxer shorts. Some can fight as well as the guys. Gay females also have longer gang careers because they don't get pregnant and drop out of gang life.

An Increase in Female Arrest Rates

Among juveniles, the rise in arrest rates for violent offenses by females was greater than that for males between 1987 and 1997. Indications are that the trend continues.

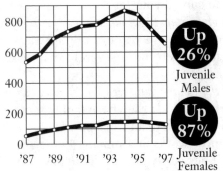

*Arrests per 100,000 juveniles aged 10–17.
Source: Federal Bureau of Investigation.

Terry Carter, *ABA Journal*, November 1999.

So getting pregnant curtails gang activity.

Biology is destiny in the gangs. For Latinas, one way out of the gangs without being punished is to get pregnant, because girls who have babies and continue to run around on the streets are looked down upon. I'd say the majority of girls I interviewed are now mothers. Once a girl became pregnant, they would try to find work and try to change their mind-set. They want to give their children a better life than they had, but they often can't get out of their neighborhoods.

But some girls wanted to be in gangs, even with children.

Right. Two of the girls I know lost their babies from an initiation rite known as the "jump-in" when you are beaten by three to five people for the count of 50.

Entering and Exiting Gang Life

What other initiation rites did you observe?

Sometimes you need to prove yourself by committing a particular crime. Then there are sexual initiations. Sometimes at a party a girl would be drunk or have something spiked and she would agree to have sex with maybe three guys but then five more would jump in. She would have no recourse because what is she going to say to the police? "I said yes to three but not to eight"? There isn't much sympathy for these girls, because getting into a gang by having sex is considered the coward's way in because all you have to do is lie back and spread your legs.

What if a girl wants to get out without getting pregnant?

If you decide to leave you must endure a "jumping out" where you are beaten more severely than when you were initiated.

Do any of the women you met go on to have careers?

Most are mothers. If they have family members that can care for their kids, they can work part-time. One of the girls in the book now works at a nursing home and another one at a factory. They really take pride in making it.

You've been criticized for changing the names of the girls you interviewed because people said they couldn't verify the stories.

I changed the names for two reasons: First, these girls were admitting to criminal activity and they weren't going to tell me anything if I used their real names. Secondly, girls tend to grow out of criminal activity sooner than boys, so I felt it wasn't fair to stigmatize teenage girls for the rest of their lives. I had two researchers working with me and we tried to verify everything we could either through police records or by talking to other kids. When I couldn't verify an incident, I tell the reader.

Gang Girls Are Devalued

What was the most disturbing thing you personally found while writing the book?

How devalued the girls were. Male gang members would sometimes demand that girls have sex with a rival gang member just to get more information on them. If the female refused, because she didn't know the guy or because she just didn't want to do it, she could be beaten for insubordination. They were in a real Catch-22 situation.

This devaluation wasn't just in gangs, but in big urban high schools, too. So many girls were suffering and no one was paying attention. I don't think a lot of these girls would have become so violent if one person along the way had listened to them or taken them seriously. But they were invisible. They looked around them and saw that the only people who received attention were boys who were beating on people. So they would emulate that.

| *"The stereotype of girls becoming gun-toting gang robbers is simply not supported by statistics."*

Girl Gangs Are Not a Growing Problem

Kim Pate

Girls are not committing greater amounts of gang violence, maintains Kim Pate in the following viewpoint. She notes that girls do sometimes commit violent crimes but asserts that it is often in reaction to violence done against them. Pate argues that the Canadian criminal justice system ignores the needs of young women and asserts that inaccurate claims about female violence fuel panic and legitimize the belief that women need to be controlled. Pate is the executive director of the Canadian Association of Elizabeth Fry Societies, which works with women and girls involved with the justice system.

As you read, consider the following questions:

1. According to Pate, when did law enforcement begin to acknowledge crimes committed by women?
2. How are young women disproportionately disadvantaged, in the author's opinion?
3. According to the author, what is reinforced by the legal system?

Reprinted, with permission from the author, from "Young Women and Violent Offences: Myths and Realities," by Kim Pate, *Canadian Woman Studies*, vol. 19, nos. 1 and 2 (Summer 1999), pp. 39–43. (References in the original have been omitted from this reprint.)

S ome time ago I received a call from a reporter asking me whether I would be prepared to do an interview with him about the increase in violent offending by young women. "What increase?" was my response. He said his local police source had advised him that their community had seen a 200 per cent increase in robbery offences alone over the past decade. When I asked him how many actual cases those figures represented, he was not certain.

Further investigation revealed that two young women had been charged with robbery—one about ten years earlier, the other had just occurred. Prior to that, there were apparently no charges or convictions of girls or young women on record. So, technically, the statistic was correct. The impression created by the 200 per cent figure and the accompanying media hype, however, created an incredibly skewed and inaccurate picture of young women suddenly erupting into violent behaviour. The reality was that the violent behaviour that was perceived to be erupting was pretty much nonexistent and the risk posed to the public by the two young women involved was incredibly low.

Inaccurate Hypotheses

I have received other calls from reporters, students, and other members of the public requesting information about the increasing number of girls in gangs. A review of the media accounts leaves one to conclude that the most common causes of this apparent phenomenon are women's desire to be equal to men and the breakdown of the family, which has resulted in girls not having their fathers around to help socialize them. The facts do not support either hypothesis.

It is interesting to note that up until the 1970s, the occasional violent acts committed by women were generally ignored by law enforcement authorities worldwide. During the '70s, a new mythology emerged that linked the women's movement to a new wave of violent offending by women. White, adult women, as leaders of the women's emancipation movement, were identified as causing the surge in serious criminal offending by women. American author Meda Chesney-Lind calls this the "liberation" hypothesis. She further says that in the 1990s, we are in the midst of a second wave that causally links women's equality with girls'—especially poor, minority girls—participation in gangs.

Throughout both "waves" there have been no significant changes in the levels and patterns of girls' violent and aggressive behaviour in Canada, the United States and the United Kingdom. There are, however, marked differences in external responses to violent or aggressive actions, especially those perpetrated by youth. The development of so-called zero tolerance policies have resulted in increased policing and prosecuting of all forms of violence committed by boys and girls. Proportionately, because the overall number of young women charged with violent offences remains relatively low, the increased numbers create more substantial percentage increases in the statistics for girls than they do for boys.

In addition, there has been an increased criminalization of young women's survival skills. In the past, it was relatively easy to institutionalize or enforce social controls on young women if they ran away, missed curfew, engaged in sexual activity, or displayed behaviour that might be defined as "unfeminine" or, worse yet, unmanageable. Under the old *Juvenile Delinquents Act*, a young woman could be imprisoned in a juvenile home for such activities. The introduction of the *Young Offenders Act (YOA)* in 1982 was supposed to end the arbitrary detention of young women for such activities. However, the way the *YOA* is being implemented by police and judges belies its legislative intent. We fear that the new *Youth Criminal Justice Act* will not rectify this situation if only the law, and not the practices, change.

The Young Offenders Act

It is now more than 15 years since the *Young Offenders Act* was proclaimed into law and paraded internationally as one of the most innovative and progressive legislative responses to juvenile justice. Since its inception, however, the legislation has had its most progressive elements gradually chiselled away.

The *YOA* is based on youth-positive principles and it is distressing to observe continued attempts to erode its fundamental tenets and guiding principles. Regressive changes have failed youth and further marginalized many youth with special needs, particularly young women.

The *YOA* calls for the least restrictive interventions possible for young people. In fact, it calls for an examination of all other youth-serving systems (such as education, child welfare, and children's mental health) prior to invoking its provisions. Alternative or diversionary options are entrenched in the act. Paradoxically, the 1990s has seen just the opposite result. In many schools or group homes, for instance, matters that would previously have been dealt with by an internal administrative authority are increasingly likely to be referred to the juvenile justice system.

A Change in Charges Against Girls

Girls are involved in more violent crime than they were a decade ago; their murder arrest rate is up 64 percent, for example. Still, violent crimes accounted for only 3.4 percent of girls' arrests in 1994. Changes in the way girls are charged, as opposed to the commission of more violent crimes by girls, may explain part of the increase in arrests for violence. For example, a girl who, in self-defense, shoves her parents out of the way as she tries to run away is now likely to be arrested for assault, a criminal offense; previously, she would have been arrested for the lesser status offense of running away. Nevertheless, status offenses (considered offenses only because the perpetrator is a minor), such as running away, prostitution, or curfew violations, continue to comprise most of girls' arrests, possibly because of a public tendency to sexualize girls' offenses and attempt to control their behavior.

Jeanne Weiler, *Clearinghouse on Urban Education Digest*, May 1999.

Rather than adopt a "zero violence" approach, "zero tolerance" policies are resulting in ever-increasing numbers of disenfranchised youth being jettisoned out of schools and communities, and usually through, rather than into, a thinning social safety net. Rather than nurturing our youth, we are increasingly scapegoating and disposing of them as though they are expendable human refuse. Statistics reveal that there has been an overall reduction in youth crime generally, as well as a relatively low incidence of violent and repeat youth crime more specifically.

These figures notwithstanding, police, reporters, and communities continue to blame the *YOA* for crime, quickly criminalize the behaviour of young people, and throw them to the wide, expensive, and ineffective net of the juvenile justice system.

Young people are best served by supportive and proactive interventions, as opposed to the punitive and reactive approaches characterized by and endemic to criminal justice responses. . . .

Young Women Are Disadvantaged

All young people suffer as a result of the lack of adequate support services and other systems-based deficiencies. Those who work with young people will be all too familiar with the erosion of resources and support for our community-based support systems for youth. The relatively small numbers of young women who are criminalized and enter the system, as compared to young men, result in even fewer services for young offenders in any community.

Young women are disproportionately disadvantaged as a result of a lack of gender-focused community and institutional programming and services, and extremely limited access to open custody settings. The majority of young women who receive open custody dispositions must serve their sentences in secure custody and/or co-ed correctional facilities. Girls and young women also tend to have more limited access to the services and programs, both in the community and in institutions. In many young offender centres across the country, incidences of sexual assault and/or pregnancies during custody have led to the further segregation of young women in correctional facilities. Young women are in real need of women-centred approaches in the youth justice system, their needs are often ignored or at best subsumed by those of young men.

Staff also cite a complete lack of resources for young women in terms of job training (in the community or institutions), education with daycare for teenage mothers, or parenting programs. In addition, there are no provisions for pregnant teens within the institutions. Lack of medical staff also places limitations on the movement of pregnant youth to camps or open custody facilities.

The overrepresentation of young women in custody for administrative breaches (such as the non-payment of fines) and child-welfare type concerns (such as child neglect) are further indicators of systemic bias. Canadian, American, British, and Australian studies of youth court charges and sentencing reveal that young women are disproportionately and overwhelmingly charged and imprisoned for administrative breaches, non-criminal behaviour, and non-status offences (such as traffic violations).

Of the very few who are arrested for crimes of violence, most of the situations involve young women reacting to violence perpetrated against them, or offences which were previously labelled as status offences that have now been reclassified as serious offences as a result of "zero tolerance." Obviously, we all wish to see a decrease in the use of violence in our communities. Criminalizing youth does not diminish violence, it merely legitimizes it in the hands of the state.

Bias and Discrimination

Young women appearing before the courts tend to have fewer charges against them than males. Systemic bias and discriminatory practices undergo a multiplier effect where gender, race, class, ethnicity, and/or sexual orientation converge. The stereotype of girls becoming gun-toting gang robbers is simply not supported by statistics. That does not mean that there are not specific and egregious examples of young women committing violent offences. It does mean, however, that every time one such incident occurs, journalists and talk show hosts beat the bushes for other examples to support extreme interpretations of the event. Police officers, teachers, social workers, criminologists, and others asked to supply "expert" opinions have a responsibility to present an accurate picture when they choose to comment in such circumstances.

In a discussion of the current focus on girls as gang members and gang leaders, Meda Chesney-Lind succinctly frames the issues and our challenges:

> As young women are demonized by the media, their genuine problems can be marginalized and ignored. Indeed, the girls

have become the problem. The challenge to those concerned about girls is, then, twofold. First, responsible work on girls in gangs must make the dynamics of this victim blaming clear. Second, it must continue to develop an understanding of girls' gangs that is sensitive to the context in which they arise. In an era that is increasingly concerned about the intersections of class, race, and gender, such work seems long overdue.

Much is already known about effective and empowering ways to meet the needs of young women. This information, combined with adequate funding for existing and innovative support services and networks, will result in more effective interventions, increased prevention and decreased recidivism. . . .

A Better Approach

There is sufficient evidence that preventative approaches to addressing crime within the context of socio-economic, gender, racial, and ethno-cultural realities are far more cost-effective than current criminal justice approaches.

Rather than see young people in either the adult or the juvenile justice system, the Canadian Association of Elizabeth Fry Societies (CAEFS) would prefer to see better services for youth in community settings. While popular in the short term, "quick fix" criminal justice responses cannot address what are fundamentally social justice and equality issues. It is far too simplistic and short-sighted to presume that the off-loading of scapegoated youth onto the criminal justice system will solve youth crime. Nor will youthful offending be eliminated by tinkering with the *Young Offenders Act* in isolation. Broader-based social reform is fundamental. Harsher sentences have not proved successful in protecting society or rehabilitating the individual.

The Department of Justice introduced Bill C-68, which proposes to repeal the *Young Offenders Act* and replace it with the new *Youth Criminal Justice Act*. Although this act aims to divert more youth from the youth justice system via extra-judicial means, it also proposes more stringent measures for youth convicted of serious and/or multiple offences. Unfortunately, so far the only new money available is earmarked for the more regressive amendments. Yet again, we are left to rely on the provinces to implement progressive elements of the Bill. Without new resources, there is faint hope that more provinces will do much to change the administration of juvenile justice in their respective jurisdictions. Hence, unless the government links its cost-sharing agreements with the provinces to the implementation of the progressive portions of the proposed new act, the *Youth Criminal Justice Act* will result in a mere rhetorical reframing of vitally important and unresolved issues pertaining to criminalized youth in Canada.

The legal system reinforces sexist, racist, and classist stereotypes of women while simultaneously legitimizing patriarchal notions of the need to socially control women. We must all commit to transforming the social and economic position of girls and women and adamantly challenge attempts to further subjugate women if we are truly interested in addressing violence in our communities. We must also refuse to fuel panic with exaggerated and inaccurate claims about increased violent offending by women and girls. Refusing to address the issues raised by the involvement of women and girls in our criminal justice system will continue to cost us much more than money.

| *"Whites are disproportionately likely to engage in all kinds of destructive behavior."*

Crimes by White Teenagers Are Not Labeled Gang Behavior

Tim Wise

In the following viewpoint, Tim Wise asserts that "gangs" is a racist term because it is only used to define minority youth. According to Wise, if the two teenagers responsible for the April 1999 massacre at Columbine High School in suburban Denver had been African American, their actions prior to the shootings would have prompted a stronger reaction and would have been labeled gang behavior. However, Wise contends, violence by whites is overlooked in discussions about crime, even though white violence poses a greater threat than crimes committed by minorities. Wise is the director of the Association for White Anti-Racist Education, based in Nashville.

As you read, consider the following questions:

1. In Wise's opinion, on what three things is black violence blamed?
2. According to the author, what percentage of the white community will be killed by a black person in a given year?
3. Why does Wise believe "Father Knows Best" and similar television shows were so popular?

Reprinted from "Blinded by the White," by Tim Wise, *Z Magazine*, June 1999, by permission of the author.

Imagine if you will the following: The place is a quiet, sub-urban community. The kind commonly referred to by its residents as a "nice place to live and raise children." It's a community known for civic pride, affluent families, and schools where the students score well above the national average on aptitude tests. It's also 93 percent white.

An Imaginary High School

Now imagine that at this community's high school, a handful of black students who say they feel like outcasts begin talking openly about how they hate everyone. They start dressing alike—perhaps wearing the same colors, or leather jackets, or black berets—and referring to themselves as the "dashiki posse."

Furthermore, they show off their gun collection in a video, which they produce for a class project. In this video, they act out the murders of dozens of their fellow students and teachers.

In addition, the students are known to operate a website which espouses hatred and violence, and on this website they have been known to post what amounts to hit lists—letting everyone know who they hate most, and intend to kill first. One of the targets of their hatred discovers the list, tells his father, and the two of them inform police of the thinly veiled threat.

Let's imagine these black students are fond of a particularly "violent" form of music—say, gangsta rap—and are known to paint viciously anti-white slogans and symbols on their clothing, and sing the praises of a particular black mass murderer—say, Colin Ferguson.

How long would it take, based on the above information, for school officials, teachers, and parents to make sure these kids were expelled from school and perhaps prosecuted? How long would it take for their families to be run out of town on a rail? Does anyone believe this scenario would have been met with apathy, cautious indifference, or even amusement?

Of course not. But that's exactly what happened when at this same school, in this same community, two white students from "good families" began dressing alike, saying they hated everyone, calling themselves the "Trenchcoat Mafia," listening to "shock-rock" and the sometimes violent lyrics of white musical artists, showing off their guns and murder fantasies on film, operating a website which praised Hitler and advocated violence, painting swastikas on their clothes, and naming the people they wanted to kill over the Internet. Still seen as "basically normal kids" by their families, friends, and teachers, these two would be ignored. Ignored that is until they went on a killing rampage reminiscent of the previous seven that have occurred at schools around the country in the past two years.

Violence and Stereotypes

"No one really thought they'd do anything," said some of their classmates. "We thought it was all talk," said others. Of course. These were white kids, with BMW's, whose families make six figures or more. These are the beautiful people. They never do anything wrong.

"We moved from the city to get away from things like this." The statement rings with a burning familiarity. It's the same thing heard after Paducah, Pearl, Fayetteville, Jonesboro, Edinboro, Springfield, and now Littleton. Some people never get it. Some people are so caught up in their race and class stereotypes about what "danger" looks like, they still insist "things like this just don't happen here."

Oh yeah? Well, where do they happen? I have yet to hear of one black or Latino kid in even one inner-city high school plotting, let alone carrying out mass murder. Just where does an urban dweller go to build 30 bombs anyway? Where can they sit around sawing off shotguns without someone noticing? Christ, if these kids had been black they would have been followed around the hardware store for so long that they would never have been able to buy any pipes, let alone the other ingredients needed for the kind of explosives Klebold and Harris used.

So in light of what's happened, not only in Littleton, but in other "nice, quiet" suburbs all around the country lately, one must ask: just what were these folks trying to get away from in the cities? Must not have been violence. Must have been black and brown people (except, of course, for the handful that can afford to live among them in style), and poor folks generally. How sad.

Once again, the racialization of crime and deviance has allowed us to let down our guard to the greatest threats to our safety: not people of color (if we're white), but our own white children, white parents, white neighbors, white husbands, white lovers, and white friends.

The Myth of White Innocence

We have been so conditioned to see deviant and destructive behavior as a by-product of melanin or "defective" black culture, that commentators can, without any sense of irony, continue to remark about how, well, remarkable it is when things like this happen.

It reminds me of something James Baldwin once said about the Holocaust—a much bigger paroxysm of white violence no doubt, but which nonetheless resonates here—"They did not know that they could act that way. But I doubt very much whether black people were astounded."

© Terry LaBan. Used with permission.

The white American myth of innocence, decency, morality, and the cowboys who never fired on an "injun" unless it was self-defense, have all been laid bare for those willing to see. That people of color always knew the myths to be bullshit, while the dominant majority refused to listen and look at themselves only makes the situation more tragic. But not a damn bit more shocking. Of course, that the mass killers in the schoolyards have all been white as of late has gone without mention in the media. Oh sure, we hear about the similarities between the Columbine High tragedy and the others—well, at least some of the similarities: all the shooters were boys; all the shooters used guns; all the shooters talked openly about violence; all the shooters played violent video games; all the shooters ate Cheerios at some point in the last ten years—you get the picture. In other words, the racial similarities between all these gun-lovin', trash-talking, dark-clothes wearing, 'Doom-playin', 'Cheerios-eatin', Marilyn Manson–listenin' bundles of testosterone are irrelevant. While we can rest assured these kids would have been "raced" had they come from black "ghetto matriarchs" in the 'hood, it seems as though no one can see the most obvious common characteristic among them: namely, their white skin. This, I guess, is what folks mean when they say they're colorblind: they can see color all right, it's white they have a problem with.

Typical, typical, typical. White folks go off, killing wholesale like there's a frickin' closeout on semi-automatic ammunition, and we get 50 zillion "explanations" from the so-called experts who are brought in by the media to make sense of it all. People of color do something horrific or commit random acts of retail violence and the whole world lines up to blame one of three things: their black families (particularly their black single mommas); their black DNA (as in the rantings of *The Bell Curve)*; or their "defective" black culture and inverted value system. Whatever the case, their blackness never gets overlooked.

White Crime Is Ignored

Gang violence in the cities heats up and we've got *U.S. News & World Report* running a cover story entitled: "A Shocking Look at Blacks and Crime," and every nighttime news program running stories asking what's wrong with the black family (as if there's only one); what's wrong with these people in the "ghetto underclass." But when Charles Manson, John Wayne Gacy, Ted Bundy, and Jeffrey Dahmer go out and do their thing, no one thinks to ask what it is about white folks that makes them cut babies out of their mothers' wombs, torture young men and bury them under the house, kill two dozen or more women for the hell of it, or consume human flesh. White deviants are afforded the privilege of individualization—"that's just crazy Charlie, ignore him, he's a potted plant"—while those of color get to represent the whole community and become exhibit A in David Duke and Charles Murray's eugenic fantasy. You say 90 percent of modern serial killers have been white? Well, isn't that puzzling. Next question.

You'll never even hear the term "white crime" uttered in polite conversation. White collar crime, maybe; but to suggest that the collar might not be the only thing lacking color, would be dogma non grata in mainstream discussion. "White-on-white violence?" What the hell is that? Never heard of it. Even in the wake of these massacres. Even as white folks are killing other white folks in Kosovo (and still other white folks are bombing them to get them to stop).

The media and politicians have done such a fine job making sure everyone knows who to fear (namely the dark and poor) that we forget how whites are disproportionately likely to engage in all kinds of destructive behavior, from drunk driving to drug use as teenagers to animal mutilation to fratricide to cutting corners on occupational safety standards and pollution control, which then result in the deaths of twice as many people as are murdered each year.

The Wrong Ideas About Crime

We forget that when it comes to violent crime, whites are four times more likely to be victimized by another white person than by a person of color, and that only sixteen-thousandths of 1 percent of the white community will be killed by a black person in a given year.

It all leads one to wonder: how many of the white families with kids at Columbine would have moved away, or at least taken their kids out of the school if, say, 50 or 100 black families had moved in and enrolled their children there? If other suburban communities and other white folks are any indication, the answer is quite a few. Study after study for 25 years has found that whites begin to leave an area and disenroll their kids from the local schools when the community becomes as little as 8 percent black. As the numbers get higher, the slow trickle becomes a mass exodus. Why? Well, to get away from crime, of course. I'm pretty sure this is the textbook definition of irony.

Even more hilarious is the tendency to act as if young white people were ever innocent, upstanding citizens compared to the rest of the country. Even as far back as 1966, a national survey of 15- to 17-year-old whites found that "virtually all" had committed numerous criminal offenses, from breaking and entering, to minor property destruction, to armed robbery.

Living in a Fantasy World

I've decided that's why all those shows like "Leave It to Beaver," "Father Knows Best," and "The Brady Bunch" were so popular: not because many people actually lived like that, but because they didn't, and could escape into this unreal fantasy life via the television. After all, why watch a program that looks just like your daily routine? That would be boring. So just as with westerns that allowed (mostly white) kids to fantasize about a more exciting life, these wholesome family programs allowed (and still allow in syndication) mostly white viewers to ignore the dysfunction which is all around them, and always has been, long before the first black kid set foot in their schools, and long before the "Godless" humanists bounced prayer from homeroom.

Unfortunately, this kind of thing will happen again. In fact, had it not been for a few folks informing on plots they knew about, we would already have added a Milwaukee suburb to the list of white teen angst killing fields, and a week after Columbine would have gotten a look at what kind of explosives Caucasians in Texas are capable of putting together. Still, according to the morning paper, less than half of all teens and their parents (mostly white if modern survey techniques are any guide) think their schools are at risk for this kind of violence.

Yeah, well, just keep telling yourself that. Keep watching "COPS" and "Real Stories of the Highway Patrol," and

"America's Most Wanted," where most of the bad guys fit the more comfortable profile to which we've grown accustomed. I can hear the dialogue now: "Why look at how menacing the large black person is honey. My, oh, my, we sure are glad we moved out here to Pleasantville. Me, my lovely wife, and our son. Speaking of whom, honey, where is Waldo anyway? I don't think I've seen him all week. Is he on that computer of his again? That scamp. Such a hard worker. Oh, and honey, what was that sawing sound coming from the garage last night?"

Periodical Bibliography

The following articles have been selected to supplement the diverse views presented in this chapter. Addresses are provided for periodicals not indexed in the *Readers' Guide to Periodical Literature*, the *Alternative Press Index*, the *Social Sciences Index*, or the *Index to Legal Periodicals and Books*.

Angie Cannon	"Kids Just Say No to Violence," *U.S. News & World Report*, November 1, 1999.
Terry Carter	"Equality with a Vengeance," *ABA Journal*, November 1999.
Adrienne D. Coles	"Federal Report on Gang Increase Met with Caution," *Education Week*, April 22, 1998. Available from Suite 100, 6935 Arlington Rd., Bethesda, MD 20814.
Congressional Digest	"Juvenile Crime: 1996–97 Policy Debate Topic," August/September 1996.
Chandra Czape	"And When She Was Bad . . . ," *American Legion*, January 1997. Available from 5561 W. 74th St., Indianapolis, IN 46268.
Tiffany Danitz	"The Gangs Behind Bars," *Insight on the News*, September 28–October 5, 1998. Available from 3600 New York Ave. NE, Washington, DC 20002.
Economist	"The Trouble with Gangs," January 16, 1999. Available from PO Box 58524, Boulder, CO 80322-8524
Ted Gest and Victoria Pope	"Crime Time Bomb," *U.S. News & World Report*, March 25, 1996.
Edward Humes	"Can a Gang Girl Go Straight?" *Glamour*, March 1996.
Issues and Controversies On File	"Teen Gangs and Crime," February 9, 1996. Available from Facts On File News Services, 11 Penn Plaza, New York, NY 10001-2006.
Steve Lopez	"The Mutant Brady Bunch," *Time*, August 30, 1999.
Adam Miller	"Gang Murder in the Heartland," *Rolling Stone*, February 22, 1996.
Bruce Shapiro	"Behind the (Bell) Curve," *Nation*, January 6, 1997.

CHAPTER 3

Can the Criminal Justice System Reduce Gang Violence?

Chapter Preface

Federal, state, and local governments use the criminal justice system to carry out policies intended to reduce gang crimes, such as imposing curfews on minors. Critics of such strategies maintain that police tend to show bias in their efforts to end gang violence—contending, for example, that police are more likely to arrest minority youth than white youth for curfew violations.

One criminal justice tool that has been tainted by possible police bias is the implementation of injunctions to regulate gang behavior. Injunctions target known and suspected gang members in specific neighborhoods and bar them from behaviors such as gathering in public and carrying pagers. Gang members who violate an injunction are arrested.

However, the future of injunctions in the Los Angeles neighborhoods of Pico-Union and MacArthur Park is questionable. In September 1999, an investigation in the Los Angeles Police Department revealed that nearly seventy alleged members of the 18th Street gang named in the injunctions were accused of gang membership based, in part, on the sworn declarations of officers who are under investigation for corruption. In addition to allegedly falsifying evidence and testimony, some officers in the antigang unit allegedly shot and beat suspects. Both injunctions were suspended to allow authorities to investigate those officers, an investigation that has continued into spring 2000. Nonetheless, many people in law enforcement continue to see injunctions as a viable approach to reducing gang violence even though some of the actions taken against gang members have been discredited by police corruption. In November 1999, Los Angeles City Attorney James K. Hahn filed an injunction for the Harbor City neighborhood.

Debates on the role of the criminal justice system in reducing gang violence often turn to the issue of whether an apparently effective policy, such as gang injunctions, is tainted by police corruption or bias. In the following chapter, the authors evaluate various criminal justice strategies.

"[Authorities must] make it clear to gangs that violence *would draw . . . crackdowns."*

The Criminal Justice System Can Reduce Gang Violence

David Kennedy

In the following viewpoint, David Kennedy asserts that the criminal justice system can deter gang violence if the appropriate methods are used. According to Kennedy, the traditional approach to deterrence is not especially successful. However, he argues that the Boston Gun Project, a criminal justice program that seeks to deter violent behavior by dealing with gangs directly, has been effective in reducing gang violence. He contends that program succeeds because it establishes clear standards for gang behavior and imposes immediate criminal sanctions on gangs that engage in violence. Kennedy is the director of the Gun Project and is a senior researcher at Harvard University's John F. Kennedy School of Government.

As you read, consider the following questions:

1. What has been "the main engine for creating deterrence," as explained by Kennedy?
2. According to the author, what percentage of youth homicides in Boston was committed by gang members?
3. How has communication with gangs changed the balance of power, in Kennedy's view?

Excerpted from "Pulling Levers: Getting Deterrence Right," by David Kennedy, *National Institute of Justice Journal*, July 1998.

More than 20 members of the Intervale Posse, a street gang in Boston's Roxbury neighborhood, are arrested in an early-morning sweep after a nearly 9-month investigation. Fifteen of the arrestees face Federal drug charges and 10-year minimum mandatory sentences; many face even stiffer sanctions. In the weeks after the arrests, Boston's Ceasefire Working Group—composed of frontline members of the Boston Police Department's gang unit, the departments of probation and parole, the U.S. Attorney General's and county prosecutor's offices, the Office of the State Attorney General, school police, youth corrections, social services, and others—meets with gangs around the city, goes to youth detention facilities to talk with inmates, and speaks to assemblies in Roxbury public schools. The message Ceasefire members deliver is simple and direct:

> The city is not going to put up with violence any longer. We know who's behind the gang violence. We're warning gangs to stop; if they don't, there are going to be consequences. There are people here who want to help you—we can offer services, job training, protection from your enemies, whatever you need—but the violence is going to stop. The Intervale Posse was warned, they didn't listen, and they're gone. This doesn't have to happen to you. Just put your guns down.

Successful Deterrence

Can we make deterrence work? Criminal justice agencies have always tried, but the results—whether of preventive patrol or the death penalty—have always been dubious. [Situations in] Boston, Lowell [Massachusetts], and Minneapolis highlight a new approach to crafting deterrence strategies, and in the larger tales that lie behind them there is reason to be optimistic. In Boston, youth homicide fell by two-thirds after the Ceasefire strategy was put in place in 1996. In Lowell, youth assaults declined; according to Lowell High School headmaster William Samaras, who had been dealing with gang conflicts among students, there was "an immediate quieting effect on the school." In Minneapolis—one of several Midwestern cities that had experienced an increasing homicide rate—homicide fell by 45 percent citywide in the months after the city kicked off its homicide prevention strategy with the Bogus Boyz' [a Minneapolis street gang] arrests. None of these operations were controlled experiments, and a detailed evaluation of the Boston intervention is still under way. But the experiences to date are interesting enough to support an exploration of the basic crime-control logic that was applied to the work in Boston, Lowell, and Minneapolis and that is currently being explored in a number of other jurisdictions.

The basic approach was developed in Boston as part of the National Institute of Justice-supported Boston Gun Project, an attempt to bring problem-solving policing to bear on the city's youth homicide problem. A two-part intervention—the Ceasefire strategy—emerged from the Gun Project's research and planning phase. One part mounted a direct law enforcement attack on the illicit market that was supplying youths with firearms. The other part was what the Gun Project's interagency working group eventually came to call a "pulling levers" strategy: deterring violent behavior by chronic gang offenders by reaching out directly to gangs, setting clear standards for their behavior, and backing up that message by "pulling every lever" legally available when those standards were violated. The deceptively simple operation that resulted made use of a wide variety of traditional criminal justice tools but assembled them in fundamentally new and different ways. It may be that the basic "pulling levers" logic can be applied in a variety of settings and against a range of different crime and public safety problems. And it may be that "pulling levers" can, where applicable, substantially alter the balance of power between the authorities and offenders.

Traditional Deterrence Is Flawed

Criminal justice has sought to generate deterrence in a variety of ways: police agencies through patrol and rapid response, probation and parole agencies through supervision, prosecutors and judges by focusing attention and sanctions on repeat and violent offenders, and the like. The main engine for creating deterrence, however, has been the basic case-processing mechanisms of the criminal justice process: the apprehension, prosecution, and sanctioning of offenders. In this model, deterrence is generated by the threat that an

A Greater Commitment to Juvenile Justice

Deterring delinquency and reducing youth violence require a substantial, sustained investment of financial and human resources by both the public and private sectors. If this Nation truly intends to ensure public safety and reduce youth violence and victimization, it must make a greater commitment to a juvenile justice system that holds juvenile offenders immediately accountable (before they become hardened criminals) and responds appropriately to the issues that bring young people to the courtroom in the first place. All young people should be guaranteed the opportunity to be healthy, safe, and able to learn in school and to engage in positive, productive activities. This requires the targeted and coordinated use of new and existing resources.

Sarah Ingersoll, *Juvenile Justice*, September 1997.

---

offender will face a formal penalty for the crime he has committed. We calculate—and presume that offenders calculate—this threat on the basis of the expected costs, imposed by the criminal justice process, on offenders for the crimes that they commit. Unfortunately, both scholarship and everyday experience suggest that the deterrent power of this strategy has not been great. It is not hard to see why. Most crimes are neither reported to nor observed by the police; in many types of crimes, such as drug dealing and prostitution, both parties to the transaction actively strive for concealment. And the majority of crimes that are reported do not result in an arrest. In 1994, 12,586,227 offenses were known to the police; only 21.4 percent were cleared by arrest. When police make an arrest, it generally takes some time for the case to make its way through to a disposition. In 1992, the average number of days between arrest and conviction for felony cases disposed by State courts was 173. Finally, most of the resulting sentences are not terribly severe; it is estimated that 52 percent of all *felony* convictions result in probation. Traditional probation is the most extensively used sanction in the correctional system. About 60 percent of offenders under correctional supervision are on probation. And while research has repeatedly suggested that the certainty and swiftness of sanctions matters more than their severity, most of the political and policy debate has centered on increasing sanctions. Debates center on the death penalty and three-strikes laws, not on clearance rates for violent crimes or the workloads of prosecutors and judges.

The resulting weakness of deterrence is perhaps particularly vexing where chronic offenders are concerned. It has long been known that a relatively small number of criminals offend at very high rates, are repeatedly arrested and sanctioned, and—if only by virtue of their continued offending—demonstrate a particular resistance to both deterrence and rehabilitation. This is a particular problem where violent offending is concerned. Not all chronic offenders are violent offenders, but a large proportion of violent crimes are committed by chronic offenders, who commit not only crimes of violence but also property crimes, drug crimes, disorder offenses, and the like. Such offenders are themselves victimized at very high rates. Boston Gun Project research, for example, showed that youth homicide was concentrated among a small number of serially offending gang-involved youths. Only about 1,300 gang members—less than 1 percent of their age group citywide—in some 61 gangs were responsible for at least 60 percent, and probably more, of all the youth homicide in the city. These gang members were well known to authorities and tended to have extensive criminal records.

The Boston Approach

Deterring violence by this group of chronic offenders became a central Gun Project goal. The "pulling levers" strategy the Gun Project Working Group designed was built on a simple but crucially important realization: Chronic offending made these youths, and the gangs they formed, extremely vulnerable. Authorities had a large and varied menu of ways—"levers to pull," as the Working Group came to call them—they could impose costs on these gangs. They could disrupt street drug activity, focus police attention on low-level street crimes such as trespassing and public drinking, serve outstanding warrants, cultivate confidential informants for medium- and long-term investigations of gang activities, deliver strict probation and parole enforcement, seize drug proceeds and other assets, ensure stiffer plea bargains and sterner prosecutorial attention, request stronger bail terms (and enforce them), and even focus potentially severe Federal investigative and prosecutorial attention on, for example, gang-related drug activity.

This was, of course, not news to the authorities. There were two problems: It was impossible to give all the gangs this kind of heightened attention all the time, and occasional crackdowns, while useful in the short term, had little long-term impact. The ability to deliver overwhelming crackdowns, however, was not in doubt. The Working Group's innovation—again, simple but important—was to make it clear to gangs that *violence* would draw such crackdowns and then *continue to communicate* with gangs as the resulting strategy unfolded.

This changed the game rather dramatically. From a world in which the cost to a gang of committing a homicide was, perhaps, that a gang member would be caught and prosecuted (while "street" benefits such as a reputation for toughness accrued to the gang as a whole), the cost soared. Added to the original risk would be everything else the authorities could bring to bear: cash-flow problems caused by street drug market disruption, arrests for outstanding warrants, the humiliation of strict probation enforcement, even the possibility of severe sanctions brought by Federal involvement. Those costs were borne by the whole gang, not just the shooter. As long as the authorities were confident that they knew what gangs were involved in a particular act of violence, as they usually were, these penalties were certain; the Working Group could always figure out ways to reach out and touch particular gangs. They were also swift: Drug market disruption, increased disorder enforcement, warrant service, probation attention, and the like could be deployed within days of a violent event. Rather than an uncertain, slow, and often nonsevere response to violence, the response with the Ceasefire strategy became certain, rapid, and of whatever range of severity the Working Group felt appropriate.

Talking to Gangs

Talking regularly to the gangs served a number of purposes. Originally, the Working Group wanted to make sure that gangs knew about this new policy—so they could comply if they wished—and to tell other gangs when a gang was being punished for violence. The Working Group also wanted to make clear to gangs that while violence would bring strong attention, refraining from violence would not win them a "pass" to deal drugs or do other crimes: This was, in language the Working Group used explicitly in the gang meetings, "a promise, not a deal." Other purposes emerged as the strategy was actually implemented. One objective was to make cause and effect clear: to explain to the city's gangs that a particular drug raid, for example, was but a means to an end and was not about drugs as such but a penalty being imposed for violence. Another purpose was to bolster the Working Group's own credibility: to be able to say to gangs, in effect, "We said it, we meant it, and here's proof of that: Here's what they did, here's what we did, here's how you steer clear." Another goal was to give gangs that appeared to be on the verge of trouble a dose of what the Working Group came to think of as "retail deterrence": to reach out to them directly, one on one and face to face, and make it clear that violence would bring a strong response.

Perhaps most important, however, was that the Working Group came to realize that communication allowed the creation of a fundamentally different balance of power between the authorities and the streets. The Working Group could deploy, at best, only a few severe crackdowns at a time. But like an old-West sheriff facing down a band of desperadoes with one bullet in his gun, direct communication with gangs allowed the Working Group to say, "We're ready, we're watching, we're waiting: Who wants to be next?" And, as with the sheriff, when that message was clear and credible, not only did nobody want to be next, it was not necessary to fire the shot. So it appears to have transpired in Boston. There was one serious crackdown in May 1996, followed by another—the one described above—in August 1996. Enforcement actions of the severity of the Intervale crackdown have not been necessary since.

| "*Government responses aimed at urban teenagers who are criminally connected . . . tend to be more concerned with the crime rate itself than with the kid.*"

The Criminal Justice System Takes the Wrong Approach to Gang Violence

Joseph Marshall Jr. and Lonnie Wheeler

In the following viewpoint, Joseph Marshall Jr. and Lonnie Wheeler argue that, while the criminal justice system is seemingly successful at reducing gang violence through arrests and incarceration, it is the wrong approach for the government to take. The authors maintain that the government should focus on preventing gang crime through the improvement of urban neighborhoods. According to the authors, if the government provides job training and rids the streets of drugs and guns, inner-city youth will feel they have opportunities in life and be more likely to reject gang behavior. Marshall and Wheeler are the authors of *Street Soldier: One Man's Struggle to Save a Generation—One Life at a Time*, the book from which this viewpoint is excerpted.

As you read, consider the following questions:
1. According to the authors, what events led to talks between the Crips and Bloods?
2. What is the government's symbolic response to a drive-by shooting, in Marshall and Wheeler's opinion?
3. What do the authors demand of government?

In the summer of 1994 I was invited to join seventeen others from the Bay Area on a ten-day tour of Israel, sponsored for local community leaders by the Jewish Community Relations Council. I wasn't sure why I had been chosen for the trip, but I had never been out of the country before and was awed by the prospect of flying halfway around the world into the heart of religious history.

We arrived in Tel Aviv late on a Friday evening and went straight to the old city, Jerusalem, before our bags were unpacked. (Actually, I had no bags to unpack; mine had been waylaid in Paris.) Shabbat was beginning, and the Jews were streaming down to the wailing wall by the thousands, men on one side and women on the other; we were told that if a woman were to be caught on the men's side, she would be beaten on the spot. I was transfixed by the entire spectacle and wandered around for about an hour taking it all in and wondering, all over again, what in the hell I was doing there.

Violence and History

The question clung to me for the next several days as we received a crash course in Holy Land history, from which I learned, among other things, that Jerusalem has been conquered thirty-eight times and completely destroyed on sixteen occasions. It was plain to see that the religious significance of the city was inseparable from its bloody heritage, a biblical irony that left me pondering the essential nature of conflict. I tried to do this from the perspective of the Omega Boys Club [an educational and nonviolence program in San Francisco, founded by Marshall]. From my vantage point, Israel testified to the fact that religion, like ethnicity and in some cases a mere street address, is fundamental to identity. The protection and preservation of identity, in turn, can be found at the center of virtually every dispute involving homeland. All around the globe—in the Middle East, in Ireland, in Bosnia—the most severe regional strife has resulted when the sovereignty of one people's identity has been challenged. In San Francisco, we call that turf. In Los Angeles, where the tradition runs deeper, generations of hard combat have crystallized the two sides into Crips and Bloods.

Against the highlighted background of more than two

thousand years of war, it was the growing prospect of peace that dominated the days we spent in Israel. Yasser Arafat visited Jericho and the West Bank, which prompted a demonstration of a hundred thousand Israelis who thought their government had taken leave of its senses by receiving the Palestine Liberation Organization (PLO) leader. Meanwhile, our little group from the Bay Area met with Ariel Sharon and Yael Dayan (Moshe Dayan's daughter), both members of the Knesset, and Faisal Husseini, Arafat's point man in Jerusalem.

Our involvement in the peace process, however trivial, brought home to me the point that practically the entire world had become involved in the Arab-Israeli negotiations. Being in the Holy Lands further impressed upon me the relative smallness of the region; Israel is about the size of Delaware, one-fifteenth the size of California. Its borders are squeezed even tighter by being closed in on two sides by enemies—Lebanon to the north, Syria and Jordan on the west—not unlike the landscape of South Central, where the Eight Trays [gang], for instance, border their archrivals, the Rolling Sixties.

The Middle East Versus America

The comparisons between the Middle East and urban America thickened the more I stirred them in my head. And so did the differences. The discrepancy that hit me the hardest was the fact that whereas the world has intervened for the purpose of bringing order to the Middle East, the Crips and Bloods continue to fight their deadly fight in virtual isolation. So do the homies of Sunnydale, Fillmore, Hunters Point [three Bay Area neighborhoods], Chicago, Detroit, Newark, and East St. Louis.

Having moderated cease-fire talks between the Crips and Bloods, having observed players from Sunnydale and Hunters Point sitting side by side at the Neighborhood House, and having watched in amazement as a hundred thousand Jews protested the peace settlement with the PLO, I can say for a fact that the brothers in the 'hoods are more receptive to the concept of peaceful coexistence than are the Israelis and Palestinians. They have also taken more initiative toward that end. In the same way that political events—the breakup of the Soviet Union and the Persian Gulf War—facilitated the Israeli-Arab negotiations, the evolving Crip-and-Blood talks were precipitated by the Rodney King incident and the ensuing insurrection. The Crips and Bloods, however, have not been visited by presidents and constantly attended to by secretaries of state. They have not received hundreds of millions of dollars of aid from the United States government. They have not been near the top of political agendas around the world. Nobody helps the homies.

Urban Children Are Ignored

This is an extremely hard thing to justify or even comprehend. It's not as if the problems in the cities are a big secret. By dropping out of school, by having babies they can't take care of, by terrorizing their neighborhoods, by killing each other, the homies have been trying for years to get our attention. They've been all over the news. Some of them have even written to the president, like the nine-year-old from New Orleans named James Darby, who in April 1994 sent a letter to President Clinton pleading with him to stop the violence in the city or "somebody might kill me." Ten days later, James was murdered in a drive-by shooting as he and his mother walked home from a Mother's Day picnic.

A few months later, there was the much-publicized Chicago incident in which an eleven-year-old boy named Robert Sandifer fired a semiautomatic pistol into a group of neighborhood kids playing football and killed a fourteen-year-old girl. Robert had been arrested twenty-eight times between the ages of nine and eleven. A few days after he shot the girl, he was found dead in a pool of blood beneath a graffiti-covered underpass, and two teenagers from the same gang were arrested for his murder. The case was essentially solved, but bigger, more pressing questions remained: After being arrested twenty-eight times in two years, what in the hell was this kid doing out on the streets in the first place? What did he learn while he was in juvenile detention? Who was looking after him? Who gave a damn about him? Where was the system?

For all the attention that Robert's case attracted, and James Darby's before him, there was no mainstream national movement that took up the cause afterward. There was no special legislative session or presidential press conference. There were no new priorities declared. It was simply business as usual around America.

Our country's deafening indifference concerning its urban children has become a time-honored, practically sacred political tradition, and that was the thing that kept ringing in my ears the whole time I was in Israel. The obvious disparities that spoke to me there—the breakdowns in logic, priority, and responsibility—were not only disturbing but disorienting: If Americans are so willing to devote their effort and their money toward peace in the Middle East, why in the hell aren't they willing to do the same to achieve it in the cities of our homeland? Where is the commitment? In American terms, where is the money? The real question here is one that shouldn't even be asked but must be: Do we really want peace in our cities? The issue has been out there for a long time now, and America's silence on the subject speaks volumes. . . .

The Government's Approach to Gangs

Urban violence, however compelling on its own account, is only the most visible symptom of a contemporary disorder that plunges deep into the American anatomy. This disorder is fostered by conditions that aren't getting any damn better. And to the degree that crack cocaine, guns, and the lack of employment opportunity have conspired to drastically alter the fundamental dynamics of the black community over the last generation—to the degree that they have made this a time like no other in the urban neighborhoods of our nation—it will require an equally potent coalition to return the community to its native values. That's the only way to truly save the children.

While I hold firmly the position that the children must be saved by individuals, those three items—crack, guns, and employment—represent specific areas in which government can and must get involved. Government must spare no effort or expense in cutting off the flow of crack cocaine and punishing its purveyors; it must unequivocally rid the nation of guns; it must promote job training, public works programs, and any and all methods of putting city people to work. It must put its money where its political rhetoric is and take the kids into account.

Government Agencies' Shortcomings

Federal juvenile delinquency policy states that "sound policy for juvenile delinquency prevention seeks to strengthen the most powerful contributing factor to socially acceptable behavior—a productive place for young people in a law-abiding society" [*Federal Register*, June 30, 1997]. Such a policy is difficult to implement through programs administered by large and separate local-level government agencies.

Government programs may do well at controlling behavior external to families, such as disorder on the street through community policing; however, the fundamental operational unit of social and emotional dysfunction in children lies inside the family. A social service or law enforcement agency can't intervene effectively in socioeconomic processes embedded in a family's transgenerational history.

Government agencies do well at providing centralized social, educational, and medical services. Ironically, however, such service delivery often occurs best inside correctional facilities, where managers can be held accountable for service delivery and where the quality and delivery of services are embedded in an organizational system that's prescribed and protected by the U.S. Bill of Rights and federal courts. Service delivery on the street requires a different organizational mechanism, because a community's social, educational, medical, and vocational service agencies usually aren't well integrated. And on the street, law enforcement dominates, particularly in the case of youth gangs, and gang kids are arrested and jailed long before a community agency reaches them. Once inside the juvenile justice system, kids get lost and pushed further aside.

Mark S. Fleisher, *Dead End Kids: Gang Girls and the Boys They Know*, 1998.

In this country, government responses aimed at urban teenagers who are criminally connected—the element Omega [an educational and nonviolence program in San Francisco, founded by Marshall] so often works with—tend to be more concerned with the crime rate itself than with the kid; more concerned, that is, with making society safer than with nurturing the young man or woman. I honestly believe that there are people in high places—certainly in low places—who would rather lock up young black men, or even let them kill each other, than put forth the effort to save them. Reflecting this mentality, government programs, to a great extent, weigh in on the criminal-justice end of the continuum, reacting to the problem with more policemen and prisons. Government places its premium on *fighting* crime, not preventing it, and has created an industry to ostensibly do that. Symbolically, its response to a drive-by shooting is to tag the body, incarcerate the shooter, and recycle the bullet. In that tradition, the state's answer to crime in California has been three-strikes-and-you're-out, in which a third felony conviction automatically carries a life sentence. The young criminal's reply has been to go down shooting on the third strike, swearing, like Jimmy Cagney in *White Heat*, "You'll never take me alive."

For now, I've resigned myself to the fact that government's punitive, back-end involvement is a constant, and that the front-end work—the counseling and the nurturing—is left to the rest of us. The champions of the underprivileged—the true Americans, judging by the ideals on which the country was purportedly founded—have always been those who, like Frederick Douglass and Martin Luther King and Malcolm X, have taken the constitution at its word and made government live up to it. Now is the time for the rest of us to take up where they left off. We have to be the heroes now. Government is not going to take the lead in this struggle; it will only follow. The best we can hope for is that it will follow the heroes.

How Government Can Change

All I demand of government is what I demand of teachers and parents and counselors and citizens at large: Care. Do for the children of America's cities what you would do for the children of Israel and Palestine. Do for them what you would do for your *own* children. Move the agenda. Get involved. Do something. There is no higher priority. The measure of any society ought not to be its foreign policy or its gross national product but the way it raises its children. In that context, the prevailing commentary on our society—our government—is that we have no national youth policy. The indictment I would serve on America is that it simply hasn't put forth any meaningful effort on behalf of its young people.

While it is certainly not government's job to raise our children, what government *can* do is reconfigure the circumstances in which children are raised. For those raised in the inner cities, drugs, guns, and unemployment are circumstances. By addressing those issues, America can clean up its urban environment; it can recast the setting. That's a task I'm happy to leave for the likes of Maxine Waters and Jesse Jackson. Meanwhile, Omega's job—my job and Jack's and yours—is to work within the circumstances, whatever they are, to nurture, counsel, love, teach, and be there for the children. We have to do the job that a family can do and even a village can do but that government can't.

"*By preventing gangs from flaunting their authority, [anti-loitering] laws establish community authority.*"

Anti-Loitering Laws Can Reduce Gang Violence

Richard K. Willard

In 1992, Chicago enacted an anti-loitering law that made it a crime for gang members or anyone associated with a gang member to stay in one place "with no apparent purpose." The Illinois Supreme Court struck down the law in 1995, stating that it arbitrarily restricted personal liberties, but the case eventually reached the U.S. Supreme Court. In the following viewpoint, written as an amicus curiae brief to the U.S. Supreme Court for the Center for the Community Interest, Richard K. Willard maintains that gang-loitering laws reduce violence because they help maintain order and prevent more serious crimes. He adds that residents of high-crime areas consider these laws a moderate and effective approach to gang violence. On June 10, 1999, the U.S. Supreme Court ruled that the law was unconstitutional. The Center for the Community Interest is a national nonprofit organization that seeks to improve civic and community life.

As you read, consider the following questions:
1. What is the "quiet revolution" in modern policing, as stated by Willard?
2. In the author's view, why are conventional suppression strategies ineffective in communities that are threatened by gangs?

Reprinted from the Center for the Community Interest's *amicus curiae* brief, Richard K. Willard, Counsel of Record, submitted to the U.S. Supreme Court June 19, 1998, in the case of *City of Chicago, Illinois, v. Jesus Morales et al.*, as it appeared in the February 1999 issue of *Supreme Court Debates*.

C hicago is not alone in seeking to resist the devastating effects of gang violence. Having witnessed the failure of more traditional policing methods, many other threatened localities—from Los Angeles to Washington, D.C.—have reacted by passing a variety of innovative laws, which range from curfew measures to anti-loitering statutes to court injunctions against specific gang members. All of these measures emphasize prevention and deterrence strategies over increased criminal sanctions. In order to meet the particular challenges of increased gang violence, communities have also strongly supported constrained expansions of police discretion, to help communities reassert their own law-abiding norms.

Residents of high-crime communities are much more likely to support gang-loitering ordinances, curfews, and other order-maintenance policies, which they perceive to be appropriately moderate yet effective devices for reducing crime. Communities have implemented these policies in various ways, tailored to their particular needs, and depending on the pervasiveness of the problem.

Maintaining Order

Just as community disorder engenders increasing disorder and crime, reinforcement of [existing] community law-abiding norms engenders increasing social order and prevents more serious crime. Modern policing theory has undergone a "quiet revolution" to learn that, in cooperation with community efforts, enforcing community public order norms is one of the most effective means of combating all levels of crime. By focusing on order maintenance and prevention, advocating a more visible presence in policed areas, and basing its legitimacy on the consent of policed populations, police can most effectively prevent the occurrence of more serious crime.

New York City's experience confirms this. Today, that city has much less crime than it did five years ago. From 1993 to 1996, the murder rate dropped by 40 percent, robberies dropped by 30 percent, and burglary dropped by more than 25 percent, more than double the national average.

These drops are not the result of increased police resources, but rather more effectively applied resources. While

New York has not increased its law enforcement expenditures substantially more than other cities, since 1993, the city began to focus intensively on "public order" offenses, including vandalism, aggressive panhandling, public drunkenness, unlicensed vending, public urination, and prostitution. This focus on order maintenance is credited for much of the crime reduction.

Anti-loitering ordinances implement community-driven order maintenance policing citywide—appropriate to the extreme pervasiveness of Chicago's gang problem—but on a neighborhood scale. Preservation of neighborhood commons is essential to ensuring healthy and vital cities.

Ineffective Strategies

Gang loitering works to increase disorder. Order-maintenance policing strikes a reasonable intermediate balance between harsh criminal penalties and inaction. Conventional suppression strategies are ineffective in gang-threatened communities. Where gang activity is prevalent, individuals are more likely to act in an aggressive manner in order to conform to gang norms of behavior. When numerous youths act according to these skewed norms, more are likely to turn to crime: Widespread adoption of aggressive mannerisms sends skewed signals about public attitudes toward gang membership and creates barriers to mainstream law-abiding society, which strongly disfavors aggression.

Accordingly, policies that "raise the price" of gang activity can sometimes function at cross-purposes. If juveniles value willingness to break the law, delinquency may be seen as "status-enhancing." As penalties grow more severe, lawbreaking gives increasing status. More severe punishments may also provoke unintended racist accusation, if community minorities view harsher penalties as unfairly applied to their particular groups. Thus, any strategy dependent on harsh penalties may in fact be "at war with itself."

Why Anti-Loitering Laws Work

Strategies that instead attack public signals to juveniles' peers about the value of gang criminality are more effective. Gang anti-loitering laws do this, for example, by "authorizing police to disperse known gang members when they congregate in public places," or by "directly prohibiting individuals from displaying gang allegiance through distinctive gestures or clothing." By preventing gangs from flaunting their authority, such laws establish community authority while combating the perception that gangs have high status. As that perception weakens, so does the pressure to join gangs that youths might otherwise perceive.

A Reasonable Regulation

Local governments should be permitted to regulate loitering that harms community life. It is one thing for courts to recognize a right to stand or stroll for no reason in public. The error in the Illinois Supreme Court opinion is that it treats loitering as if it were free speech, something that can be regulated in only the most extreme cases.

As to [whether] this regulation [is] arbitrary or unreasonable—consider this analogy. In most communities it is illegal to drink alcohol from an open container in a public place. Yet most of the people who drink in public places are entirely innocent of any other wrongdoing. Does that fact render the regulation arbitrary or unreasonable? Should such an ordinance be ruled unconstitutional? Few think so. It is hardly arbitrary or unreasonable for a community to regulate an activity—even when the activity is engaged in by entirely innocent people—when that activity frequently leads to harmful consequences for others.

Roger Conner, *Responsive Community*, Fall 1998.

Such strategies also positively influence law-abiding adults. Gang-loitering laws augment law-abiders' confidence so that they can oppose gangs. When public deterrence predominates, individuals are much less likely to perceive that criminality is widespread and much more likely to see private precautions as worthwhile. When the community as a whole is again able to express its condemnation, gang influence quickly wanes.

The most successful anti-gang programs combine effective gang suppression programs with targeted community aid efforts: increased social services, job placement, and crisis intervention. Civil gang abatement, together with other government and community-based efforts, has reduced crime and visibly improved the neighborhood's quality of life.

Chicago has also implemented alternative community aid programs. Since 1992, for example, the Gang Violence Reduction Project has targeted Little Village to serve as a model gang violence reduction program.

The program coordinates increased levels of social services—the carrot—in conjunction with focused suppression strategies—the stick. The result has been a lower level of serious gang violence among the targeted gangs than among comparable gangs in the area. The project also noted improvement in residents' perceptions of gang crime and police effectiveness in dealing with it. Chicago's anti-loitering ordinance is the necessary "stick" of an effective gang violence reduction equation.

"It is . . . not clear that the anti-gang law actually benefited anyone."

Anti-Loitering Laws Are Ineffective and Biased

David Cole

In the following viewpoint, David Cole contends that anti-loitering laws, such as the one that had been instituted in Chicago, do not reduce gang violence and are unfairly directed toward African Americans. He maintains that the loitering law is not responsible for Chicago's declining crime rate. In addition, Cole asserts that the ordinance increases the distrust minorities have for police, because the target is primarily young African American men. Cole is the *Nation's* legal affairs correspondent and the author of *No Equal Justice: Race and Class in the American Criminal Justice System.* This viewpoint was written prior to the June 10, 1999, U.S. Supreme Court decision that ruled the Chicago ordinance unconstitutional.

As you read, consider the following questions:
1. What are the arguments presented by supporters of the ordinance, as listed by Cole?
2. Why does Cole question the argument that the minority community in Chicago supported the loitering law?
3. According to the author, what is the law's most powerful tool?

From "Standing While Black," by David Cole. Reprinted with permission from the January 4, 1999, issue of *The Nation.*

D o "quality of life" policing and "community" policing, the law enforcement watchwords of the nineties, require the abandonment or dilution of civil rights and civil liberties? On December 9, 1998, the Supreme Court heard arguments in a case that starkly poses that question. At issue is a sweeping Chicago ordinance that makes it a crime for gang members or anyone associated with them merely to stand in public "with no apparent purpose." Chicago calls the offense "gang loitering," but it might more candidly be termed "standing while black." Sixty-six of the more than 45,000 Chicago citizens arrested for this offense in the three years that the law was on the books challenged its constitutionality, and in 1997 the Illinois Supreme Court unanimously ruled that it violated due process.

But the Supreme Court agreed to review that decision, and lined up in defense of the ordinance is not only the city of Chicago but also the United States, the attorneys general of thirty-one states, the National District Attorneys Association, the International Association of Chiefs of Police, the US Conference of Mayors and, perhaps most interesting, a pair of otherwise liberal University of Chicago law professors representing several Chicago neighborhood groups.

Disputing the Arguments for Loitering Laws

The ordinance's advocates argue that it played a critical role in making Chicago's high-crime neighborhoods safe and therefore served the interests of the minority poor who live there. They suggest that strict constitutional standards need to be loosened in order to give police the discretion to engage in the day-to-day encounters of "quality of life" or "community" policing. Most astounding, they argue that criminal laws no longer must be clear in places where minority groups have a voice in the political process and can protect themselves. These arguments resonate with one commonly heard these days, particularly but not exclusively in Mayor Rudolph Giuliani's New York City—namely, that heavy-handed police efforts directed at the inner city benefit minority residents by making their neighborhoods safer places in which to grow up, work and live.

The arguments fail. First, as an empirical matter it is far

from clear that the minority community in Chicago supported the law or that minority communities generally favor "quality of life" policing efforts that send so many of their residents to jail. The majority of Chicago's African-American aldermen voted against the ordinance; one representative, predicting that the law would be targeted at young black men, compared it to South Africa's apartheid regime. And voter turnout rates are so low in the inner city that it is difficult to say whether any elected official speaks for that community. The notion that minorities no longer need the protection of constitutional law simply ignores the racial disparities evident at every stage of the criminal justice system.

A Better Approach

Gangs congregating in public can doubtless be a blight and a danger—blocking sidewalks, making noise, selling drugs and intimidating passersby. But the way to deal with those problems is to crack down vigorously on this kind of behavior. . . .

Taking that approach would have the advantage of focusing less on the innocent and more on the guilty.

Stephen Chapman, *Conservative Chronicle*, June 23, 1999.

It is also not clear that the antigang law actually benefited anyone, much less Chicago's minority communities. Chicago did experience a falling crime rate while the law was in effect, but so did the rest of the nation. And the crime rate continued to fall after the ordinance was invalidated. So it is far from proven that arresting tens of thousands for standing in public had any positive effects.

Law Enforcement Must Build Trust

Most important, giving the police unfettered discretion to sweep the city streets of "undesirable" youth probably undermines safety by incurring distrust among those community members whose trust the police need most. The law's most powerful tool is its legitimacy. The more people believe the law is legitimate, the more likely they are to internalize its mores, obey its strictures and cooperate with police. When laws are enforced in discriminatory ways, they lose their legitimacy. Cynicism and alienation about the criminal law are nowhere higher than among minorities and the urban poor, and laws like Chicago's only feed the alienation by inviting selective enforcement.

Indeed, law enforcement authorities and experts have long understood the importance of maintaining the community's faith and trust. Thirty years ago, the Kerner Commission reported that such support "will not be present when a substantial segment of the community feels threatened by the police and regards the police as an occupying force." The father of "quality of life" policing, George Kelling, has argued that street sweeps are antithetical to its goals precisely because they foster enmity, not community. And Attorney General Janet Reno has written that effective crime control requires "a greater sense of community and trust between law enforcement and the minority community." Yet her Justice Department, the City of Chicago and the majority of our nation's state attorneys general fail to understand that you don't build trust by unleashing the police on minority communities with carte blanche to arrest anyone standing in public without an apparent purpose. Civil rights and civil liberties, far from impeding law enforcement, are critical to preserving its legitimacy.

| *"Community-based curfew programs that offer a range of services . . . provide a greater benefit in preventing juvenile delinquency and victimization."*

Curfews Can Help Reduce Violence

Shay Bilchik

In the following viewpoint, Shay Bilchik asserts that curfews, if implemented properly, can help reduce juvenile violence. He notes that such laws must be written in a manner that ensures their constitutionality, so they can withstand legal challenges. Bilchik contends that curfews are most likely to be effective if they are not exclusively reactive and punitive but also include proactive elements that will help prevent delinquency. Bilchik is the administrator of the Office of Juvenile Justice and Delinquency Prevention in the U.S. Department of Justice.

As you read, consider the following questions:
1. According to statistics provided by Dallas and cited by the author, when are murders by juveniles most likely to occur?
2. What are some of the common elements of most curfew programs, as stated by Bilchik?
3. According to Bilchik, what are some auxiliary benefits of community-based curfew programs?

Excerpted from "Curfew: An Answer to Juvenile Delinquency and Victimization?" by Shay Bilchik, *Juvenile Justice Bulletin*, April 1996.

Traditionally, the determination of a minor's curfew has been considered to be a family issue, within the parental purview, rather than a matter to be determined by government. Nevertheless, public curfews have been enacted and enforced throughout the Nation's history in reaction to increased juvenile delinquency, decreased parental supervision, and other social trends. Recent increases in juvenile crime and victimization have prompted local communities in many States to once again consider evening curfews (e.g., from 11 P.M. to 6 A.M. on school days and from midnight to 6 A.M. on nonschool days) as a viable means to enhance the safety of the community and its children. Although most curfew ordinances apply to juveniles under 16 years of age, some include 16- and 17-year-olds. This viewpoint explores developments in curfew ordinances, legal issues related to curfews, how jurisdictions have responded to legal challenges, the elements of sound community-based curfew programs, and examples of a range of curfew programs and services from seven jurisdictions.

In a recent study of curfew ordinances in the 200 largest U.S. cities (population of 100,000 or greater in 1992), William Ruefle and Kenneth Mike Reynolds found a dramatic surge in curfew legislation during the first half of the 1990's. Of the 200 cities surveyed, 93 (47 percent) had curfews in effect on January 1, 1990. Between January 1990 and the spring of 1995, an additional 53 of these 200 cities (27 percent) enacted juvenile curfew ordinances, bringing the total of those with curfew laws to 146 (73 percent). During the same period, 37 of the 93 cities with an existing curfew ordinance revised that legislation.

The question of curfews has raised a variety of legal issues and divided numerous communities, as the following sample of newspaper headlines illustrates: "The Trouble with Curfews," "Cities Deciding That It's Time for Teen Curfews," "Curfew Not a Good Idea," "Curfew Needs to Be Stronger," "Limiting Kids' Time on the Streets Elicits Both Relief and Resentment." Differences in opinion have led individuals and civil rights organizations in many communities to challenge the legality of juvenile curfew ordinances. The American Civil Liberties Union (ACLU), the most vocal opponent, has challenged the constitutionality of juvenile curfew ordinances in jurisdictions across the country, either directly or by providing assistance to individuals who wish to test such laws in court. . . .

The Strict Scrutiny Test

In order to pass constitutional muster, laws that impinge on fundamental constitutional rights must pass a two-pronged strict scrutiny test that requires jurisdictions to (1) demonstrate that there is a compelling State interest and (2) narrowly tailor the means to achieve the law's objective. The Dallas curfew provides an excellent example of an ordinance that has been held by a Federal court to satisfy both prongs of the strict scrutiny test.

The Dallas City Council adopted its curfew ordinance in 1991 after hearings that included testimony on increased incidences of late-night juvenile violence. Challenged by the ACLU, Dallas' curfew ordinance was upheld in 1993 by the U.S. Court of Appeals for the Fifth Circuit in *Qutb v. Strauss*. The Fifth Circuit held that the Dallas curfew satisfied the strict scrutiny test because the city had demonstrated a compelling State interest in reducing juvenile crime and victimization and because the ordinance was properly aimed, that is, narrowly tailored to ". . . allow the city to meet its stated goals while respecting the rights of the affected minors." A subsequent appeal was refused by the Supreme Court of the United States without comment in May 1994. However, this ruling neither guarantees protection from future constitutional legal challenges to curfews in other circuits under the provisions of the U.S. Constitution or State constitutions, nor forecloses challenges based on nonconstitutional grounds.

Statistics Show That Curfew Is Needed

Jurisdictions that seek to enact curfew laws may want to examine how Dallas laid the groundwork needed to pass the strict scrutiny test. Data on juvenile crime and victimization helped meet the compelling State interest test. The city provided the following statistical information:

• Juvenile delinquency increases proportionally with age between the ages of 10 and 16 years.

• In 1989, Dallas recorded 5,160 juvenile arrests, and in

1990, there were 5,425 juvenile arrests, including 40 murders, 91 sex offenses, 233 robberies, and 230 aggravated assaults. From January through April 1991, juveniles were arrested for 21 murders, 30 sex offenses, 128 robberies, 107 aggravated assaults, and an additional 1,042 crimes against property.

- The most likely time for the occurrence of murders by juveniles was between 10 P.M. and 1 A.M.; the most likely place was in apartments and apartment parking lots and on streets and highways.
- Aggravated assaults by juveniles were most likely to occur between 11 P.M. and 1 A.M.
- Rapes were most likely to occur between 1 A.M. and 3 A.M., and 16 percent of rapes occurred on public streets and highways.
- Thirty-one percent of robberies occurred on public streets and highways.

The Court relied on these data in holding that the City of Dallas provided sufficient evidence to establish that the ordinance was in keeping with the State's compelling interest in reducing juvenile crime and victimization.

Second, the Dallas legislation was narrowly tailored to address the specific needs enumerated by the jurisdiction by the least restrictive means possible. The Dallas curfew was applied to youth under the age of 17 and in effect from 11 P.M. through 6 A.M. Sunday through Thursday and from midnight to 6 A.M. Friday and Saturday. The statute exempted juveniles who were:

- Accompanied by an adult.
- Engaged in activities related to interstate commerce or protected by the first amendment.
- Traveling to or from work.
- Responding to an emergency.
- Married.
- Attending a supervised school, religious, or recreational activity.

The Fifth Circuit found, in *Qutb v. Strauss*, that the exemptions under the Dallas ordinance, which permitted juveniles to exercise their fundamental rights and remain in public, demonstrated that the ordinance was narrowly tailored to meet the city's legitimate objectives.

Other Curfew Requirements

Other challenges to juvenile curfews have been based on the concepts of vagueness and overbreadth. A statute is void for vagueness if it is too general and its ". . . standards result in erratic and arbitrary application based on individual impressions and personal predilections" [*Bykofsky v. Middletown*, 1975]. A statute that broadly restricts fundamental liberties when less restrictive means are available may be void on the grounds of overbreadth. Therefore, when constructing juvenile curfew ordinances, in addition to considering constitutional issues that involve fundamental rights, jurisdictions should ensure the legislation is both precise in its language and limited to necessary restrictions.

In addition to constitutional and structural challenges to juvenile curfews, jurisdictions enacting curfew laws should also bear in mind the core requirement of the Juvenile Justice and Delinquency Prevention (JJDP) Act of 1974, as amended, which addresses the deinstitutionalization of status offender and nonoffender juveniles (DSO). In general, this JJDP Act core requirement prohibits a status offender (i.e., a juvenile who has committed an offense that would not be a crime if committed by an adult, such as truancy or curfew violations) or nonoffender (i.e., a dependent or neglected child) from being held in secure detention or confinement. However, Office of Juvenile Justice and Delinquency Prevention (OJJDP) regulations allow detention for brief periods in a juvenile detention facility—not to exceed 24 hours exclusive of weekends and holidays—necessary for pre- or postcourt appearance, processing, release to a parent or guardian, or transfer to court or an appropriate nonsecure facility. The statute also makes exceptions that allow the detention or confinement of status offenders who violate a valid court order or who violate State law provisions prohibiting the possession of a handgun. Status and nonoffender juveniles cannot be detained or confined in an adult jail or lockup for any length of time. To comply with the DSO core requirement of the JJDP Act Formula Grants Program, and to reduce the burden on police, Dallas and many other cities have established comprehensive, community-based curfew programs that provide local sites, such as community and recreation centers, where police officers can bring curfew violators for temporary detention pending release to their parents or other appropriate disposition. These sites provide an atmosphere conducive to investigation, processing, prerelease counseling, and planning for appropriate followup services. . . .

A Judge's Ruling

The District [of Columbia]'s curfew regime is unquestionably rationally related to its goals of reducing juvenile crime and violence. By requiring that minors in public during curfew hours be accompanied by an adult, the D.C. Council reasonably assumed that adults will normally protect minors in their care and prevent them from victimizing others. In addition, the experience of other jurisdictions facing increases in juvenile crime and victimization indicated to the D.C. Council that a curfew can be a useful tool in fighting such problems. Reports on the specific experiences of Dallas and San Antonio, Texas, and New Orleans, Louisiana, showed that after a juvenile curfew became effective, the number of juvenile arrests for violent offenses decreased, and the Dallas and San Antonio reports also showed reductions in juvenile victimization. . . .

Testimony before the D.C. Council further confirms that the Act is rationally related to the governmental interest in reducing juvenile crime and victimization. From the law enforcement community, the D.C. Council heard, through a representative of the Community Branch of Community Policing who has taken "ride-alongs" with the Metropolitan Police Department, that the juvenile curfew is "an important tool," although "not an all-inclusive cure," because "it disrupts the gang activity, the drug trade, the hanging out waiting for the right opportunity to commit the crime. It also removes potential drive-by victims from public places where they can be targets."

Judith W. Rogers, *Tiana Hutchins v. D.C.*, May 22, 1998.

Each [city] has its own unique and innovative approach to addressing the problem of juvenile crime and victimization through a curfew ordinance. The approaches demonstrate a range of community partnerships and nonpunitive strategies designed to promote early intervention to prevent the development of delinquent behavior and to address the issues of parental responsibility, discipline, and family dysfunction. The strategies have been credited with helping to prevent juvenile crime and victimization and repeated curfew violations while providing protection and safety to the community.

While the comprehensive, community-based curfew programs . . . employ a variety of strategies, each program includes one or more of the following common elements:

• Creation of a dedicated curfew center or use of recreation centers and churches to receive juveniles who have been picked up by the police for violating curfew.

• Staffing of curfew centers with social service professionals and community volunteers.

• Intervention, in the form of referrals to social service providers and counseling classes, for the juveniles and their families.

• Procedures for repeat offenders, including fines, counseling, or sentences to community service.

• Recreation and jobs programs.

• Antidrug and antigang programs.

• Hotlines for followup services and crisis intervention.

The cornerstone . . . is creative community involvement that works to transform the juvenile curfew from a reactive, punitive response to a proactive intervention against the root causes of juvenile delinquency and victimization. . . .

The Benefits of Curfews

Community-based curfew programs that offer a range of services are more easily and effectively enforced, enjoy community support, and provide a greater benefit in preventing juvenile delinquency and victimization. In addition, several of the benefits of positive interventions that community-based curfew programs can provide may not be easily quantifiable—at least in the short term. Phoenix curfew staff have observed that many of the curfew violators brought into the recreation centers that function as curfew reception centers welcome the opportunity for social interaction with other youth and with program staff. Often these youth seek advice, assistance, and counsel from program staff. Parents sometimes bring their son or daughter to a curfew site to seek assistance and advice on the best approach for curfew compliance or to deal with other problem behaviors.

Communities that develop and implement curfew ordinances in conjunction with programs and services designed to assist youth and families to solve underlying individual or family problems have an opportunity to enhance positive youth development, prevent delinquency, and reduce the victimization of children.

"There is no evidence that sending 142,000 kids through the justice system each year for staying out too late reduces crime."

Curfews Do Not Reduce Violence

Vincent Schiraldi

Curfews do not reduce juvenile violence, claims Vincent Schiraldi in the following viewpoint. Schiraldi, the director of the Justice Policy Institute, argues that an analysis of curfews in California shows that those curfews did not lead to significant declines in crime. Schiraldi contends most crimes by juveniles are committed during the afternoon and evening, not late at night when the curfews are in effect. In addition, he maintains that such laws are unfair to law-abiding children, especially minorities. The JPI is a project of the Center on Juvenile and Criminal Justice, a private organization whose mission is to reduce society's reliance on the use of incarceration as a solution to social problems.

As you read, consider the following questions:

1. By what percentage did arrests for curfews increase between 1994 and 1996, as stated by Schiraldi?
2. According to the author, in the first year of New Orleans' curfew, how many more black youths were arrested for curfew violations, compared to white youths?
3. What does Schiraldi believe is the strongest argument against curfews?

Reprinted, with permission, from "Curfew's Time Has Passed: System Not a Factor in Controlling Youth Crime, Statistics Show," by Vincent Schiraldi, published on the Center on Juvenile and Criminal Justice's website at www.cjcj.org/jpi/legal092899.html.

The District of Columbia once again has a youth curfew and many people—from Mayor Anthony Williams to Metropolitan Police Chief Charles Ramsey to child advocates—are touting it as an effective means to control juvenile crime with little downside.

Before the last two decades, curfews were generally thought of as temporary measures, enacted during times of crisis like natural disasters or civil unrest. But youth curfews, now in effect in about 300 cities, have become a way of life in America, despite dubious public safety benefits and evidence of unfair enforcement.

Curfews Do Not Reduce Crime

When most Americans think of youth crime today, they immediately think of children fleeing bullet-ridden schools. But more children are arrested for curfew violations each year than for any other offense. In 1996, there were 142,433 juvenile curfew arrests, up 116 percent since 1994. This compares with 97,809 arrests for burglary (down 16 percent) and 39,037 for robbery (down 18 percent). In fact, the number of kids arrested for curfews outnumbers all juvenile arrests for violent crimes, combined. Yet there is no evidence that sending 142,000 kids through the justice system each year for staying out too late reduces crime.

[In 1998] my organization conducted a comprehensive analysis of curfews in California. We analyzed curfew enforcement in California's 12 largest counties between 1978 and 1996 as well as curfew enforcement in 21 cities with populations greater than 100,000 in Los Angeles and Orange counties from 1990 to 1996. If curfews were a successful crime control policy, counties and cities with stricter curfew enforcement would be expected to have experienced more precipitous drops in juvenile crime than those with no curfew or lax enforcement.

The findings were distinctly disappointing for curfew supporters. For the entire state of California, there was no category of crime (misdemeanors, violent crime, property crime, etc.) that significantly declined in association with youth curfews. Overall, counties with strict curfews witnessed no decrease in youth crime relative to counties without strict curfews.

In four large counties (Los Angeles, Santa Clara, Fresno, and Ventura), there was evidence of racial bias in curfew enforcement. Latino and African-American youths were arrested for curfew violations at rates several times higher than that of white youths.

The counties of San Francisco and San Jose are approximately 40 miles apart and serve as an interesting point of comparison. Following an incident in which a black youth was arrested for a curfew violation while several nearby white youths of similar age were not, San Francisco all but abolished its curfew laws. While San Jose had 311 curfew arrests between 1996 and 1997, San Francisco had none. Yet both cities witnessed a nearly identical decline in their juvenile felony arrest rates.

We do not have to look to California for an example of how curfew laws fail to correlate with public safety. Since the D.C. curfew law was suspended in 1996, the number of juvenile homicides in the District has dropped by almost 50 percent, from 23 to 12.

Why Curfews Fail

How is it possible that curfews, which make so much intuitive sense—who can be against kids coming home on time?—can fail to affect juvenile crime? For one thing, the next time your car gets broken into, think about the police officer who could have been cruising past your car but was spending a couple of hours transporting a curfew violator to a police station and filling out paper work. When police are drawn away from real law enforcement to chase kids committing no other crimes but staying out late, public safety is compromised.

Second, the District of Columbia's curfew, like most around the country, kicks in at a time of day when juvenile crime is already on the decline. The city's curfew bars anyone under 17 from staying out past 11 P.M. on school nights, and past midnight on weekends. Studies show that crime by young people peaks sharply from 3 P.M. to 8 P.M.—after school closes and before parents get home. It then declines dramatically in the evening hours.

Finally, as sad as this is to say, curfews can sometimes put children in harm's way by forcing them to be home at times when they might be better off out of doors. Some of the abused kids my organization works with say they just know when dad has come home on a drunken binge that it is a good idea to get away for a little while until things calm down. Curfews would make that sensible, albeit temporary, alternative a crime.

The issue of disparate enforcement also should be of particular concern for a city whose juvenile detention facility has a population made up entirely of African-American teenagers on most evenings. No one—be they a curfew supporter or opponent—can seriously contend that a group of 16-year-old white youths on the way back from the Uptown movie theater in northwest D.C. will be treated the same as a group of 16-year-old black youths walking back from the Anacostia Metro station after an overtime Wizards [professional basketball] game.

Racial Disproportion

In the first year that New Orleans implemented its curfew, 19 times as many black youths were arrested for curfew violations as white youths. One 12-year-old boy was arrested on the way home from a McDonald's restaurant with his two teen-age sisters. When his foster mother was unavailable to pick him up, the boy was shackled to eight older, African-American boys who had also violated curfew and taken to a police lock-up. Unable to contend for one of the few mattresses in his cell, he spent the evening sleeping on the floor.

If middle-class white kids were arrested at 19 times the rate of African-American youths, there would be no debate over the effectiveness of the New Orleans curfew, because there wouldn't be a New Orleans curfew—period.

The African-American youth I work with in a counseling program in Anacostia already feel as though they have a bull's-eye painted on their backs. They don't need another reason to feel alienated from law enforcement.

Government Intervention Is Not Helpful

In a September 12, 1999, commentary in the *Washington Post*, child advocate Elizabeth Siegel equated allowing one's children to stay out after midnight with neglect and expressed hope that law enforcement involvement would help flush out some neglectful parents.

I'll be the first to admit that I occasionally stayed out past curfew—yes, sometimes even past midnight—when I was 16. Sometimes I got away with it, but mostly, there was hell to pay and a series of consequences to suffer. My parents and I had to deal with one another as I tugged against their supervision and they, against my desire for unfettered freedom. In retrospect, I consider that struggle a natural evolution that teen-agers go through with their parents—one in which the government has no place. I can't imagine that the intervention of the state into what was essentially a parent-child issue would have helped anyone.

Juvenile Crime Peaks in the Afternoon

Percent of serious violent incidents in age group

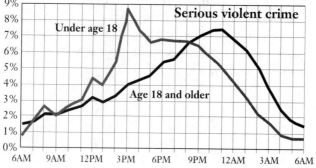

The FBI's *National Incident-Based Reporting System* master files for the years 1991–1996.

This is especially true in the District of Columbia where the state is hardly a benign instrument. The district's child welfare system, which Siegel hopes will intervene in the lives of these "neglectful" parents whose kids break curfew, has been under a federal receivership for the past three years. In other words, D.C. itself has been found to be a neglectful parent.

It is bad enough that kids who are truly abused and neglected have to be thrust into such a system. But let's not expand that net any further to kids whose only crime is staying out too late.

Generally, courts are unwilling to take constitutionally guaranteed rights from Americans unless there is a strong showing that it is necessary to achieve an important public safety goal. But as we have already seen, crime by juveniles declines during the curfew hours, crime by D.C. juveniles was already falling without a curfew, and cities that enforce curfews do no better at controlling crime than cities that do not have curfews.

Most Murderers Are Adults

The curfew thus violates kids' and parents' rights unnecessarily. But the curfew is not just wrong because it's an infringement on constitutional protections, it's also bad public policy. Ninety-two percent of the homicides in America last year occurred at the hands of an adult, while less than one-half of 1 percent of America's children were arrested for a violent crime of any kind last year.

We shouldn't teach our kids that their rights may be clipped uniformly because of the crimes of a handful. That is, perhaps, the strongest argument of all against the District of Columbia's curfew.

Periodical Bibliography

The following articles have been selected to supplement the diverse views presented in this chapter. Addresses are provided for periodicals not indexed in the *Readers' Guide to Periodical Literature*, the *Alternative Press Index*, the *Social Sciences Index*, or the *Index to Legal Periodicals and Books*.

Craig Aaron   "Menaces to Society," *In These Times*, December 13, 1998.

John Allen   "U.S. Teens Face Rash of Get-Tough Actions as Nation's Fear Grows," *National Catholic Reporter*, January 10, 1997. Available from 115 East Armour Blvd., Kansas City, MO 64111.

David C. Anderson   "When Should Kids Go to Jail?" *American Prospect*, May/June 1998.

Paul M. Barrett   "FBI's Antiviolence Campaign in Los Angeles Is Again Raising Issue of Racial Discrimination," *Wall Street Journal*, February 1, 1996.

Geoffrey Canada   "Curfews Are for Parents to Set," *New York Times*, July 23, 1996.

Roger Conner   "Rights for Gangs, Handcuffs for Neighborhoods," *Responsive Community*, Fall 1998. Available from 714 Gelman Library, George Washington University, Washington, DC 20052.

Susan Estrich   "Defining Criminal Behavior," *Liberal Opinion Week*, July 5, 1999. Available from PO Box 880, Vinton, IA 52349-0880.

Evan Gahr   "Towns Turn Teens into Pumpkins," *Insight on the News*, February 3, 1997. Available from 3600 New York Ave. NE, Washington, DC 20002.

John Gibeaut   "Gangbusters," *ABA Journal*, January 1998.

Marcia Slacum Greene   "Connecticut's Remedy: Isolate and Reprogram Members," *Washington Post National Weekly Edition*, October 7–13, 1996. Available from 1150 15th St. NW, Washington, DC 20071.

Sarah Ingersoll   "The National Juvenile Justice Action Plan: A Comprehensive Response to a Critical Challenge," *Juvenile Justice*, September 1997. Available from 810 7th St. NW, Washington, DC 20531.

Randall Kennedy   "Guilty by Association," *American Prospect*, May/June 1997.

Tanya K. Metaksa	"Attacking Gangs, Not Civil Rights," *American Rifleman*, November/December 1997. Available from the National Rifle Association of America, 11250 Waples Mill Rd., Fairfax, VA 22030-9400.
Daniel J. Sharfstein	"Gangbusters: Enjoining the Boys in the 'Hood," *American Prospect*, May/June 1997.
Nina Siegal	"Ganging Up on Civil Liberties," *Progressive*, October 1997.

CHAPTER 4

How Can Society End the Threat of Gangs?

Chapter Preface

In 1991 a group of former felons living in the District of Columbia formed the Alliance of Concerned Men. Since that time, the alliance—whose goal is to end the cycle of violence and hopelessness among troubled youth in the nation's capital—has garnered praise and media attention, most notably after a gang truce it helped establish in 1997.

In January 1997, twelve-year-old Darryl Hall was beaten, abducted from the Simple City housing project in Washington, D.C., and then shot by three teenagers who were reportedly members of the Circle gang. The alliance, in an effort to prevent retribution murders—Hall was allegedly associated with the Circle gang's rival, the Avenues—brought the gangs together. Two weeks after Hall's murder, a truce was declared. Since that time, Simple City has seen only one homicide, which police believe was not gang-related, and violence in the neighborhood has dropped significantly. With the aid of David Gilmore, receiver for the D.C. Housing Authority, the alliance helped turn Simple City youth away from gang life by providing them with jobs such as landscaping and renovating the housing projects. In addition to these jobs, gang members began to complete their high school education or earn equivalency diplomas, with some continuing on to college.

Robert L. Woodson Sr., president of the National Center for Neighborhood Enterprise and the host of the first truce meetings, contends that the Alliance of Concerned Men has been able to reach out to gangs because its members were involved in gangs and crime during their own adolescence. He writes in the *Wall Street Journal*: "Neighborhood-based, grassroots groups, led by committed individuals who have personally experienced the problems they address, know how to instill vision and hope in young people others have labeled as 'hopeless.'"

The neighborhoods where gang violence has caused the greatest problems have taken a variety of approaches to reducing the threat of gangs. In the following chapter, the authors consider how society might best end the dangers posed by gangs.

"Gang schools . . . must be at the center of the community's attention if the gang problems are to go away."

Schools Can Help Reduce the Problem of Gangs

Arturo Hernandez

In the following viewpoint, Arturo Hernandez asserts that schools can reduce gang violence by providing mentoring and encouragement to gang members. Schools can let these "bad kids" know that they matter to the community, he maintains, by providing services such as support groups, cultural and athletic opportunities, ties to local businesses, and ceremonies that acknowledge their accomplishments. Hernandez, who has founded two experimental schools for gang-involved youth, is the author of *Peace in the Streets: Breaking the Cycle of Gang Violence*, from which this viewpoint is excerpted.

As you read, consider the following questions:
1. According to Hernandez, which group benefited most from the Scared Straight tour?
2. In Hernandez's view, what advantages do "good kids" receive?
3. What is the impediment to "bad kid" schools, in the author's opinion?

Reprinted from chapter 3 of *Peace in the Streets: Breaking the Cycle of Gang Violence*, by Arturo Hernandez. Copyright ©1998 Child Welfare League of America, Inc. Used with permission from the Child Welfare League of America.

S everal years ago, I participated in a version of the Scared Straight program. In this particular case, I went with the students from one of the local high schools. On this special day, the top Latino students toured a local university to motivate them toward college. The troublesome students toured the local youth camp, one of the places to which juveniles are sentenced, the idea being that this would motivate them away from delinquency.

The show delivered. Students marched through corridors and listened to screaming inmates; they looked in tiny cells with exposed toilets. One girl behind a metal door gave a haunted-house shriek and cried for the passing students to come join her. Then the inmates gave presentations.

The first, a huge Mexican boy, looked at our males and asked, "Are you from Santa Barbara?" They answered by nodding slightly. "Good. The last boy from Santa Barbara turned into my toy. I'll be waiting for you." Another inmate described the toilet situation and told the group that here their humanity would be lost. They would have no privacy, wipe themselves in front of other prisoners, never be able to do one thing without permission and observers. A young woman talked about missing her friends and mother and how she wished she could do it all over again.

What effect did this have? On the students, no more than a good, scary movie. They talked about it at McDonald's in the same excited voices they would use if they had attended a gory slasher film. It was theater, and they knew it. But that's not the point.

Helping Juvenile Inmates

The tour did have a powerful positive effect, but not on those students it was intended to impress. The real value resided in what this project did for the inmate team that produced the program. To be a presenter in this effort, juvenile inmates had to show exemplary behavior and be role models to other inmates. They had to memorize their scripts and go over them critically with the officer in charge of the program. After each presentation, the officer and the other volunteers rated their delivery, gave advice, and offered congratulations.

This program involved a lot of extra work for these incarcerated volunteers, yet they received nothing in return. Absolutely nothing. They did not get time off their sentences, extra goodies, money, or a chance to go home. Nothing. Instead, they were actually scrutinized closer than other inmates and punished more severely for infractions. But they loved the program, and they loved the officer in charge.

For these incarcerated youth, the opportunity to be special, to accomplish something, to have a coach and mentor, to be part of a winning team meant everything. It also provided a structure, supportive peers, skills, a caring mentor, recognition and reprimands, and continuous feedback. It provided all of these daily, and right where the kids lived. Combined with the regular schooling provided at the youth authority, the addition of this program gave these adolescents the training, support, and direction they needed as kids becoming adults.

The youth authority camp was not having this powerful impact on the other delinquents. The other juveniles did not experience the attentive eye of an adult with a plan for them, they did not have a peer group that felt like a team, and their victories were not celebrated.

Just as the first step is for a community to see these children, so the second must be to support and create places that provide the daily education, mentoring, direction, encouragement, and help that these kids require. This community place must be where the kids belong, it must be close to home and part of the neighborhood, and it must be a place with a plan. For the Scared Straight inmate team, they found a place with a plan inside of the youth camp.

But what happens back in the neighborhood? Who takes the torch? Where do these teens go to control their addictions, get support and references when applying for their first jobs, learn to read, have hyperactivity or a learning disabilities diagnosed, or find athletic teams to participate in? These inmates are still teenagers; they have miles to go, and unless the local community has a plan for them, they won't make it.

"Bad Kid" Schools

Once a community has taken a vow to acknowledge, support, and keep track of all its children, including the "bad ones," then it must acknowledge, support, and keep a keen eye on the places where these "bad kids" will be served and transformed. Gang schools, opportunity rooms, or wherever else a child-raising community decides to gather its wayward children, must be at the center of the community's attention if the gang problems are to go away.

I know it irks people to celebrate the accomplishments of "bad kids." Read the Bible and the story of the prodigal son. The "good kids" will do well in this world. They receive our praise, our trophies, our financial aid packages, our trust, and our jobs; everything we have is theirs. But the "bad kids" come home to us with nothing, and we have to let them know that they count. We have to let them know that we are glad they are home. This means a few fireworks and a little extra attention.

A Teacher's Perspective

Whereas kids often fall into gangs almost unconsciously, they stay out of them only by choice. But it isn't easy. "It's messed up out there," Antonio Soto, a former student, told me recently, reflecting on the three years that had passed since he'd left Seward. "Everybody's trying to be hard. If they see you're soft, they'll try to take advantage of you. Jack you up, steal stuff from you. So it's like you got no choice. You gotta be hard, too." It is the same philosophy schools and teachers often fall back on when trying to deal with students who are in gangs. We respond to kids who have become hardened by trying to be even harder ourselves.

But . . . I have learned that it is possible to take a hard-line stance on the institution of gangs without turning my back on kids who are gang members. Acknowledging them and giving them opportunities to thoughtfully reflect on their experiences in the classroom may help them become equipped to make better choices. It can enable them to see alternative realities, to envision other futures for themselves. It can present possibilities for growth, for change.

Greg Michie, *Rethinking Schools*, Winter 1997/1998.

We do want to solve this problem, right? Then we need to provide "bad kid" schools with
- small student-teacher ratios, with well-trained aides;
- ties to the business community to provide each delin-

quent a chance to learn how to apply and interview for jobs and how to work;

• weekly support groups—led by teachers, probation officers, or counseling interns from local colleges—aimed at meeting individual goals, such as sobriety, attendance, getting to work on time, and not breaking probation;

• ties to cultural and athletic opportunities, both with local high schools and with recreation centers and other sponsors;

• visits from local court judges who sentence these youths, to encourage them and let them know that everyone is working together to keep them on track;

• parent support groups;

• field trips to colleges, junior colleges, training centers, and other places that we want to make familiar so students feel at ease visualizing themselves attending there;

• access to specialists who can diagnose learning problems and emotional difficulties and suggest remedies and resources;

• well-publicized rituals and ceremonies marking the small, but important accomplishments of these students. A newspaper group photograph, a certificate, a good word to a parent could all acknowledge such accomplishments as attending class 80% of the time, meeting important academic goals like reading improvement, maintaining sobriety for a certain number of months, not breaking probation, or obtaining a job and keeping it. Each brick counts. Celebrate so that it sets well.

Transforming the Schools

There are many examples of schools that currently try to do this, and they succeed with little funding and scarce attention. I am familiar with the Soledad Enriched Action Schools of East Los Angeles, the Expeditionary Schools of Santa Barbara County, and the Desert Eagle Charter School on the Salt River Reservation. There are probably hundreds that I don't know about. The impediment is not that these schools are rare; the problem is that they are invisible and seen as peripheral to the job of educating a community's youth.

The small "bad kid" schools that most school districts sponsor don't have football teams or booster clubs. They are seen as transitory places. This is wrong. They must be schools that are alternatives for kids—many, many kids—who need the intimate structure of such schools to succeed. We need to be as aware of what these schools do and the resources that they need as we are of our regular secondary schools.

All of this takes money, but not much more than we already spend. The most significant difference will be that, instead of these schools being invisible and without much respect, they will become sources of attention and pride in their communities.

In your community, how many kids need this kind of a school? What does your local "bad kid" school need to educate every gang member on probation, every gang member who is feeling defeated in regular school? What do they need to successfully make every such student a confident, competent adult?

Imagine if they succeed in this task.

> "We now know that [school-based] programs put America's at-risk youth at even greater risk."

School-Based Programs Are an Ineffective Response to Gang Violence

Elizabeth J. Swasey

School-based programs such as midnight basketball do not decrease juvenile crime and gang violence, Elizabeth J. Swasey asserts in the following viewpoint. She cites assaults and murders committed by youths that participated in these programs as proof that such strategies are ineffective. Swasey notes that even an evaluation by the U.S. Justice Department has concluded that these programs do not reduce juvenile crime. Therefore, she argues, Congress should not increase funding for these programs. Swasey founded the women's personal safety program at the National Rifle Association and is the director of the NRA's CrimeStrike, which works to improve the criminal justice system.

As you read, consider the following questions:
1. How does Congress define "at-risk youth," according to Swasey?
2. By what percentage did juvenile arrests for murder increase between 1985 and 1995, as stated by the author?
3. According to "Preventing Crime: What Works, What Doesn't, What's Promising," what crime-prevention strategies do reduce crime?

Reprinted, with permission, from "At-Risk of 'Prevention,'" by Elizabeth J. Swasey, *American Guardian*, October 1997.

Syracuse, New York—Henninger High School, July 24, 1995, 8:45 P.M. Police officer Michael Sales and corrections officer Romie Days were off-duty, working security at the local version of Midnight Basketball called "Midnight Madness."

Violence by At-Risk Youth

It was Monday night. The championship game was set for Thursday. Suddenly, some of the "at-risk" youth in the Henninger High School gym started a fight. Officers Sales and Days took the perpetrators outside. Once outside, violence erupted among another group of youths. Fists started flying. Then a few cars pulled up, and more young people piled out. Some joined the fights already underway; others started their own.

The intersection of Teall Avenue and Robinson Street had become the scene of a street brawl. Officer Days, 43, saw two young men point guns straight at him, then shoot. Days fired back but the suspects escaped, speeding away from the "crime-prevention program" at Henninger High School.

San Fernando, California—October, 1985. Karen Severson and Michelle "Missy" Avila, both 17, attended the San Fernando Mission, which wasn't a mission at all. Instead, it was a "Continuation School" which at-risk youth are required to attend after committing crimes. There, students get intensive academic instruction as well as programs in job skills, parenting, arts and crafts, and music and dance.

Karen, Missy, and Laura Doyle were friends who "liked to party." They were on the way to their favorite hangout in Colby Canyon when Karen and Missy began arguing over a boy they had both dated. The argument got heated, and then got out of control. Karen and Laura turned on Missy, attacking her, cutting off her hair, forcing her face-down into a creek. They held Missy's head under eight inches of water and used a log nearly as long as Missy was tall to pin her body down. Missy died where she lay.

Unsuccessful Programs

When it comes to juvenile crime, crime-prevention programs are designed for at-risk youth, which Congress defines as people ages 11–19 who have dropped out of school or committed a crime of any kind, or who might drop out of school or commit any kind of crime.

And believe it or not, both the Midnight Madness and Continuation School "crime-prevention programs" are, by Congressional measure, "successful."

For the last quarter century, Congress has measured crime-prevention programs not by their results, but simply by whether the program was put into place—something Congress calls the "process objective."

But if these are crime-prevention successes, what is failure?

With any luck, what we call a successful program is about to change—and none too soon. We're nose-to-nose with a national crisis. Juvenile arrests for murder are up 115% from 1985 to 1995. Even so, things are poised to get worse.

Judging Success

By 2006, America's teenage population will exceed 20 million for the first time since 1975, a demographic inevitability that Princeton University criminologist John J. Dilulio, Jr., calls the "youth crime bomb." He warns of a violent juvenile crime explosion that Northeastern University criminologist James Alan Fox says is "really, really possible."

Even President Clinton agrees that cutting juvenile violent crime must be our top crime-fighting priority.

As a result, it's no longer enough for Midnight Basketball to be called a "successful crime-prevention program" simply because two teams are playing hoops at designated hours, or for a school-based, at-risk youth program to be called a "successful crime-prevention program" simply because it has enrollment.

To judge success, we must know whether rival gangs use Midnight Basketball games to settle violent scores, or whether Continuation School students use their camaraderie to kill. We must know if they work. And for the first time, we're beginning to get answers.

In 1996, Congress required the U.S. Attorney General to provide a "comprehensive evaluation of the effectiveness" of the over $3 billion—that's billion with a B—that the Department of Justice grants annually for crime-prevention. The research had to be "independent" and had to "employ rigorous and scientifically recognized standards and methodologies."

Why Some Activities Do Not Reduce Crime

Some programs offer recreational, enrichment or leisure activities as a delinquency prevention strategy. These programs historically have been based on one of the following assumptions: (1) "idle hands are the devil's workshop"; (2) children—especially those who do not fit the academic mold—will suffer from low self-esteem if they are not able to display their other competencies; or (3) "students need to vent their energy. With the rise in violent crime, the typical rationale for alternative activities programs is that occupying youth's time will keep them out of harm's way—the "safe haven" theory. Drop-in recreation centers, after-school and week-end programs, dances, community service activities, and other events are offered as alternatives to the more dangerous activities. After-school programs have enjoyed a recent boost in popularity in light of evidence that 22% of violent juvenile crime occurs between 2 P.M. and 6 P.M. on school days. This is more than would be expected if juvenile crime were uniformly distributed across the waking hours.

Relevant research on alternative activities is found both in basic research on the causes and correlates of delinquency and in evaluations of prevention programs involving these activities. Basic research has examined the plausibility of the "idle hands is the devil's workshop" rationale for explaining delinquency and found it lacking. Several studies have found that time spent in leisure activities is unrelated to the commission of delinquent acts. Time spent on activities which reflect an underlying commitment to conventional pursuits (e.g., hours spent on homework) is related to the commission of fewer delinquent acts, while time spent on activities which reflect a (premature) orientation to adult activities (e.g., time spent riding around in cars) is related to the commission of more delinquent acts. But the myriad activities of adolescents that have no apparent connection to these poles (e.g., clubs, volunteer and service activities, youth organizations, sports, hobbies, television, etc.) are unrelated to the commission of delinquent acts. Simply spending time in these activities is unlikely to reduce delinquency *unless they provide direct supervision when it would otherwise be lacking.*

Denise C. Gottfredson, "School-Based Crime Prevention," from *Preventing Crime: What Works, What Doesn't, What's Promising.* www.ncjrs.org/works/index.htm.

This evaluation is now out. It's a 500-page report called "Preventing Crime: What Works, What Doesn't, What's Promising." It judges crime-prevention success not on whether the program is put in place, but by whether it cuts crime.

School-Based Programs Have Failed

According to "Preventing Crime," school-based programs intended to "keep the most crime-prone segment of the population off the streets during peak crime hours . . . and to enhance positive youth development through mandatory attendance at workshops covering topics such as job development, drug and alcohol use, safe sex, GED preparation and college preparation, and conflict resolution" are "not likely to reduce crime." In fact, the report says, these programs "may actually increase risk for delinquency [criminal behavior]."

Yet if President Clinton and his allies in Congress have their way, there'll be even more of these programs to come—even though they put at-risk youth at even greater risk by increasing crime, or by squandering millions on programs that are "not likely to reduce crime" when we should be investing taxpayer funds where they can make a difference.

True to its name, "Preventing Crime: What Works, What Doesn't, and What's Promising" does report that some crime-prevention strategies cut crime. Among them, incarcerating repeat offenders—including juvenile offenders.

This is the research. These are the facts. And it's likely that some of the same politicians who called for this report, especially Senator Joe Biden (D-DE) and Congressman Charles Schumer (D-NY), will wish they hadn't. But the fact is, the Clinton-Gore Biden-Schumer approach to the crisis of violent juvenile crime has been school-based crime-prevention programs, and we now know that these kinds of programs put America's at-risk youth at even greater risk.

So the next time the President asks, in support of his pet "prevention" programs, "Who can be against allowing a child to stay in school instead of on a street corner?" we can provide the answer: Criminologists hired by your own Justice Department.

"Breaking the cycle that leads youths to criminal behavior requires an effort on all our parts."

The Community and Law Enforcement Must Work Together to Reduce Gang Violence

Roger Quintana

In the following viewpoint, Roger Quintana asserts that the police and the community, particularly parents, need to work together to reduce gang violence. He argues that suppression efforts—such as targeting and arresting gang members—should be left to law enforcement. However, Quintana contends, the police, schools, government agencies, and citizens can cooperate in intervention and prevention strategies to dissuade children from joining gangs. According to Quintana, parents also can help keep their children out of gangs by teaching positive values. Quintana is a youth crime prevention specialist in Boise, Idaho.

As you read, consider the following questions:
1. What is "tough love," as defined by Quintana?
2. According to Quintana, when is the most critical time of day for children?
3. What two rules should parents follow, in the author's view?

Reprinted, with permission, from "Your Child, My Child, Our Child," by Roger Quintana, *Community Links*, Winter 1998. For more information on this topic, contact the Community Policing Consortium at 800-833-3085.

The consensus about who is responsible for the condition of our youths, for the rise in youth gangs, drugs, violence and crime is an often unattractive, unyielding, unchanging and inaccurate debate. Those who deny responsibility for the negative behavior displayed by so many youths are outnumbered by those of concerned and understanding citizens who accept that none of us are exempt, and are all called to positively influence America's children and young adult populations.

Prevention: It's Everyone's Responsibility

Prevention begins at home. If the stove is hot, the child is advised not to touch it; but if he or she does, a wise parent first comforts, then disciplines. This approach is part of what some feel is the emotional roller-coaster coined "tough love." The strategy is one that requires much from the caregiver and must consistently be applied throughout a child's early and middle years to yield unshakable character. Through initiatives led by local schools, government agencies, police, political and community groups, as well as a contingent population of concerned citizens, a community can stay on top of its youth gang, drug, violence and crime problems. Prevention is the key to maintaining a positive and structured environment for not only the at-risk youth population but for all school-aged children.

Intervention Effects Change

Intervention strategies can be effectively used to educate gang members, their associates, marginal players and youths flirting with the idea of gang affiliation or drug use such as alcohol, tobacco or other controlled substances. Intervention initiatives should include the school, community, and parent and youth populations, and be delivered through awareness education, classroom instruction, parenting programs, and youth social-development activities and programs. It is well documented that the best intervention (and prevention) tool available is "keeping children busy." The most critical time of day for children is not while they are at school but rather between the early evening hours of 3 and 7 P.M. These are the hours when the children who are left alone will participate in their own self-approved recreational activities.

DIVIDED WE FALL; UNITED WE STAND.

Used with permission from Kirk Anderson.

Suppression: The Most Controlled Phase in the War on Crime

Suppression efforts such as targeting gangs, arresting drug users and pushers, and controlling the "out-of-control," are best left to the local constabulary. These professionals are a community's enforcement tool and are trained to address and resolve dangerous and illegal activity. It is not that community assistance and/or involvement is unwanted by law enforcement, it is simply that citizen efforts are most appropriate during the intervention and prevention phases.

Who's Really at Fault?

An oft-asked question is, "Who is really responsible for the escalation of the negative youth movement in our society?" A fair reply is that to some extent, we all are. Some psychologists say that humans are genetically predispositioned to be "good or bad." That debate continues, but what we do know for sure is that values are taught; the process begins at birth and is reinforced through the environmental family orientation. Most would agree, that as a child grows, he or she acquires habits and traits through parental teaching and family design.

If a parent teaches and models positive values throughout

a child's infant and toddler years, the child is more likely to play a positive role as he or she transitions from the home to social and school environments. Children who don't have the benefit of such an upbringing may be more likely to assume negative societal roles, ones rooted in neglect or from a lack of concern. This shaky foundation leaves some children with a middle-of-the-road thought pattern, one that makes them unsure of what is right or wrong, and that so often leads to bad choices and destructive outcomes.

Cycle is the term used to describe a completed circle of events; in colloquial terms it's believing that "whatever goes around comes around." Breaking the cycle that leads youths to criminal behavior requires an effort on all our parts. Parents, however, can take the lead by adhering to a couple of simple rules. First, don't talk to your children, communicate with them. And, second, remember that respect is earned, and real love is offered and received unconditionally. Confucius once said, "Love with discipline, discipline with love." Parents need not shoulder this burden alone. We all need to remember that it takes an entire village to raise a child.

*"The most critical people in the anti-gang
effort are the parents and guardians in the
community."*

Parents and Youth Need to Become Involved in Anti-Gang Programs

Rick Landre, Mike Miller, and Dee Porter

Parents and youth must take a more active role in reducing gang violence, maintain Rick Landre, Mike Miller, and Dee Porter in the following viewpoint. They assert that parents must be aware of what their children are doing and who their friends are, should know the signs of gang involvement, and should participate in community anti-gang programs. Young people should also become involved in community activities and be aware of the consequences of gang activity, the authors contend. Landre, Miller, and Porter are the authors of *Gangs: A Handbook for Community Awareness*, from which this viewpoint is taken.

As you read, consider the following questions:
1. According to the authors, how can recalcitrant parents be encouraged to participate in anti-gang efforts?
2. What causes the cycle of gang violence, according to Landre, Miller, and Porter?
3. What are some of the consequences of gang involvement, as listed by the authors?

The most critical people in the anti-gang effort are the parents and guardians in the community. Our short list of contributing factors in promoting gang activity lists several factors that are directly connected to the home. Parental neglect, the absence of recognition, and poor role models are known to have a large impact on gang recruitment.

Steps Parents Should Take

Many parents give lip service to anti-gang efforts, but what must they do to support the community?

1. *Accept responsibility.* Parents must be parents. They should know what their children are doing in and out of school. Who are their friends, where do they go, and what do they do there? They should respond to notices of unexcused absences from school, have their children at home by a reasonable time, be a role model and demonstrate genuine concern about their children, and teach their children to respect themselves and the community.

2. *Be knowledgeable.* Parents need to know the signs of gang involvement, as well as the services available in the community to help when they suspect trouble.

3. *Support and participate.* Parents should get involved in the community anti-gang programs and offer support by volunteering time and money if possible.

Those citizens who are not parents still have a responsibility to become involved and support the three criteria listed above. No one should be sitting on the sidelines. There are those recalcitrant parents who will need to be encouraged to participate. This can be done through community effort. Parents of students with unexcused absences could serve detention and/or community service with their offspring. Failure to respond to school requests for a conference could be handled by the courts as a case of parental neglect. Placing legal pressure upon the parents to be responsible is a last resort, but one that needs to be considered. Additionally, parents of known gang members could be held accountable for their children's activities, and sent to anti-gang education programs with their children.

Following are several specific examples of how parents

and others can make a contribution to the community's gang control program.

Kennedy High School in Sacramento, California, started a program known as Parents on Campus in November of 1992 after another local high school experienced one in a series of school shootings. The parents volunteer their time to help school security patrol the campus, and are additional eyes and ears for potential trouble. Since the program started, the school has seen a 24 percent drop in reported cases of injury, while the school district had a 20 percent increase overall. Suspensions have also decreased by 28 percent compared to the district's increase of 38 percent. . . .

Joe Debbs of Sacramento decided to become a community activist when his nephew was assaulted and beaten in a savage gang attack. Debbs formed A Guard Against Narcotics and Gangs (AGANG) as a neighborhood watch program to counter the spread and influence of street gangs. Despite his efforts, his own daughter was seriously wounded in a drive-by shooting in May of 1994. The attack may have been revenge motivated.

Debbs volunteers his time to work with the Sacramento Police Department in a conflict resolution program at area high schools. He also works with youngsters one on one to help them with problems. The violence that continues to afflict his family appears only to encourage him to continue his work.

In Jackson, Tennessee, Shirlene Mercer grew tired of the gang violence that claimed 19 deaths there in 1993. She decided that community action was the only way to put an end to the violence and began weekly marches that attract between 50 and 350 participants. The community has responded, and as of September 1994 the city had recorded only four murders.

Another individual attempting to make an impact is Dave Brown in Boise, Idaho. He publishes a monthly magazine, *Wanted by the Law: America's Monthly Crime Report!* It promotes positive stories about police officers and ordinary citizens whose heroism is an inspiration to everyone. As the magazine's title proclaims, photos of the nation's most wanted criminals are also featured.

Signs of Gang Involvement

Parents or guardians should look for the following signs of their children's involvement with gangs:

- Declining grades and/or attendance problems
- Friends who are constantly in trouble at school or with the police
- Appearance of tattoos or graffiti on clothing, books, or in their room
- Use of unusual nicknames
- Appearance of unexplained items or money
- Preference for specific colors or type of clothing
- Practice and use of hand signs
- Staying away from home and out late, without permission or explanation
- Withdrawal from family
- Increase in vandalism and/or violent activity in the community, school, and neighborhood
- Use of drugs and/or alcohol
- Friends who use drugs and/or alcohol
- Possession of permanent markers or spray paint cans
- Possession of pagers by friends of children
- Unusual handwriting or drawings on books and homework
- Increase in accidents as evidenced by injuries

Preventing Gang Involvement

- Spend time with your children.
- Learn the signs of gang involvement.
- Know who your children's friends are and contact their parents occasionally.
- Know where your children go and what they do for fun.
- Go to school meetings with teachers and administrators.
- Establish and *enforce* acceptable rules and expectations for your children's behavior.
- Do not tolerate the use and/or presence of drugs, alcohol, cigarettes, or gang involvement by your children or their friends.
- Talk to your children about alcohol, drugs, and gangs.
- Listen to and respect the feelings and attitudes of your children.

- Help your children to become knowledgeable contributing citizens.
- Find or form a parent support group if you find your child involved in gangs. Contact school officials and police about your children's involvement.
- Check your children's rooms for drugs, money, and weapons.
- Ensure that your community provides adequate and appropriate recreational activities for youth and families and participate in them.
- Be a role model.
- Help your children develop regular study habits and show interest in their schoolwork.
- Give your children praise or encouragement; don't allow yourself to become too judgmental about their choices, and allow for mistakes or disagreements.
- Teach your children how to deal with peer pressure and how to say no to friends.
- Volunteer, if possible, to participate in and promote the programs that support the community's anti-gang program.

Positive Efforts by Youths

The youths of the nation have not been silent on the issue of street gangs, drugs, and violence. They are more than willing to take a stand and work to remove these threats to the community. Some have even given their lives. We hear about stories of young people killed, shot, and/or beaten for refusing to join or give into gang intimidation. Many have called hotlines to inform authorities of potential hazards and criminal behavior. Others provide positive role models in their communities and remain to help others when no alternative help is available. Even gang members themselves have become sick of the constant violence and have asked local authorities to help them call a truce between rival factions and find a peaceful way to resolve their problems.

The following are examples of how youths across the country are taking charge and attempting to make a difference.

In separate, unrelated cases, members of street gangs in Sante Fe, New Mexico, and Lima, Ohio, have asked community leaders to help them keep a truce in an attempt to stop the senseless killing. Significant is the fact that the gangs are initiating the pacts and are trying to change.

Jesse Atondo, a 16-year-old student in rural Kern County, California, gathered over 300 signatures on a petition to the board of the local elementary school district requesting them to consider and adopt a school uniform policy. Atondo's petition drive resulted in California State Senator Phil Wyman sponsoring a bill in the legislature to legally support local school districts adopting school uniforms to help keep their students safer from gang violence. The bill became law in August 1994, and many districts across the state began planning for implementation in the following school year.

Parent Education Is Crucial

Temperamental problems [in children] do not spell doom. . . . What matters is how well the parenting and educational experiences of these children meet the challenges posed by their difficult temperaments. Of special concern are two patterns. The first is a pattern of escalating conflict in the parent-child relationship, in which parent and young child get caught up in mutually coercive and aversive interactions. The second is a gradual process of emotional detachment arising when parents and teachers abandon these children by withdrawing from them in the face of their negative behavior.

These patterns of response increase the odds that these vulnerable children will become increasingly frustrated and out of sync as they meet up with the challenges of paying attention in school. In a culture like ours, in which there is such intense cultural imagery that legitimizes and models violence, this emotional abandonment is particularly dangerous. *Parent education starting before children are born and continuing through until adolescence is crucial for preventing violence.*

James Garbarino, *Lost Boys: Why Our Sons Turn Violent and How We Can Save Them,* April 1999.

In February of 1994, over 100 students staged a two-hour protest over the adoption of a dress code by Highland High School in Sacramento, California. The dress code banned hats from being worn indoors and shirts that portrayed drugs, alcohol, smoking, or sexually explicit material. Baggy pants and gang-related clothing were also banned. District officials met with the students and agreed to conduct weekly meetings and to publish a newsletter informing all district students on progress in discussion of the policy. What may have appeared to be open defiance was actually an attempt by students to have some input into the decisions affecting them directly. Better communication and student involvement would have prevented this embarrassing situation for the district and resulted in a more effective student dress code.

In Nebraska, plans for organizing youth councils in communities across the state were presented by the Cornhusker Youth Leadership Council. The council intends to travel throughout the state and help youth in individual communities set up similar councils that can give them a voice in solving problems and other community affairs. The council believes that the more that youths are involved in community affairs, the less likely they are to become a problem.

Locking up youthful gang members has not resulted in any long-term reduction in crime, only temporary reprieves while offenders are off the streets. These offenders return to the same community environment that they left, and soon pick up their old ways unless they have gained insight while incarcerated. Such insight is rare unless the juvenile has participated in education and treatment programs during incarceration. To combat this cycle, we need to refer to its causes: poverty, need for recognition, peer group pressure, poor role models, lack of opportunity, etc. We must counter these factors, which lead to gang activity, by providing education and positive alternatives.

Factors Leading to Gang Involvement

- Lack of personal identity
- Lack of appropriate alternatives and/or activities
- Peer pressure
- Need for safety/security (protection)
- Absence of parental involvement or demonstrated concern
- Membership by other family members or friends
- Substance abuse by youth and/or parents
- Lack of opportunity for recreation or employment
- Poor academic achievement
- Sporadic attendance at school

- Rundown physical environment
- Inappropriate, or lack of, role models
- Feeling of hopelessness
- Limited education opportunities
- Lack of knowledge of the consequences of gang involvement

Consequences of Gang Involvement

- Risk of physical injury, disabling injury, or death
- Constant fear of physical danger
- Probability of committing a crime as an initiation rite
- Obtaining a criminal record
- Incarceration in a juvenile and possibly an adult institution
- Permanent tattoos
- Financial hardship, emotional distress, physical injury and possibly death to family members
- Risk of AIDS from homemade tattoos

What Youths Should Do

- Accept personal responsibility for your safety and others by informing officials of potential danger.
- Support the community's anti-gang effort.
- Suggest and participate in community activities to combat gang activity.
- Don't pretend to be a gang member; it could get you killed.
- Tell the truth to parents and adults about activities. If you want trust and respect, then you must earn it.
- Keep your family informed about your activities and friends.
- Remember that adults and parents make mistakes too.

"*Gang truces . . . have had some notable successes both in stopping violence within communities and in ending interethnic violence between youth gangs.*"

Gang Truces Have Helped End Violence

Beatriz Johnston Hernández

In the following viewpoint, Beatriz Johnston Hernández asserts that gang truces, if designed properly, can reduce violence. She contends, however, that while truces may stop the killing, they do not change the economic and social conditions that led to the formation of gangs in the first place. According to Hernández, in order to eliminate gangs, violence, and drug dealing, truces must provide gang members with economic opportunities, job training, counseling, and other services. Hernández is a correspondent for *El Processo*, a magazine published in Mexico City.

As you read, consider the following questions:

1. In Hernández's view, what are some of the programs that must be implemented if cities are to provide a viable alternative to gangs?
2. According to Michael Zinzun, as quoted by Hernández, by what percentage has violence in south central Los Angeles decreased because of the truce?
3. What ironic situation has occurred in some areas that have ended youth gang violence, according to the author?

Excerpted from "Searching for Inner-City Peace," by Beatriz Johnston Hernández, *Third Force*, May/June 1996. Reprinted with permission.

The Black Panthers are gone. So are the Brown Berets. But the organizers of the gang truce movement sweeping the country are hoping that a new generation of urban guerrilla fighters will rise like a phoenix from the ashes of self-destruction.

The fourth anniversary of the watershed Watts truce [in Los Angeles]—which was forged in 1992 between the PJ Watts Crips from Imperial Courts, the Grape Street Crips in the Jordan Downs Housing Projects and the Bounty Hunters, a Bloods gang from Nickerson Garden Projects— was as much a political event as a community celebration. Organized by local activists from Communities in Support of the Gang Truce (CSGT) and other organizations, the April 27, 1996, event featured calls for participants to form work committees on union organizing, economic development, electoral politics, job creation, law and justice, and police abuse.

Social Conditions Must Be Changed

Gang truces in other areas of the country have had some notable successes both in stopping violence within communities and in ending interethnic violence between youth gangs. But truce organizers have found that stopping the violence is much easier than creating something positive in its place. Putting an end to the killing is a necessary first step, say many of the participants in gang truces, but it does not change the economic and social conditions that give rise to gangs in the first place.

Economic development programs, job training, counseling and other programs are needed on a massive scale if cities are going to be able to provide a viable alternative to gangs. Even in Los Angeles the historic Watts truce has not yet brought about a political movement capable of reversing the city's priorities, which still favor downtown development over improving conditions in residential neighborhoods.

A Variety of Truces

In places notorious for youth bloodshed—Los Angeles, Venice, Long Beach, Whittier and Rosemead, California; San Antonio and El Paso, Texas; Gary, Indiana; Chicago; Boston;

147

Denver and Philadelphia—truces have worked to stem violence. No one has precise numbers, but experts estimate that around 50 gangs, ranging in size between 250 and 5,000 members each, are engaged in some kind of peace process. There's even a truce in the California prison system between the state's northern gang Nuestra Familia and the southern Mexican Mafia.

The "vast majority of people in the five major [Black] projects of Los Angeles are participating in some form with the gang truce," says former Black Panther Michael Zinzun, now the director of the CSGT. He adds that violence has decreased by 20 percent in South Central Los Angeles as a direct result of the truce and that Black communities are becoming more mobilized. Zinzun even attributes the success of the Million Man March to the truce movement. "Most of those there were youth who had embraced truces," he says. "There were Crips and Bloods from all over the country." [A march held in October 1995. It was organized by Louis Farrakhan and brought nearly one million African-American men to Washington, D.C.]

Truce organizers say breaking the cycle of attack and revenge starts with finding a common ground of humanity. In Watts there were two series of talks, one at an Islamic temple, the other at football star Jim Brown's home.

Meetings in Watts

Gitu Sadicki of a Los Angeles–based violence prevention program remembers the meetings at the temple. "In this place, a neutral zone, the guys could cry about their pain, the loss of loved ones," Sadicki says. "The Imam allowed them to discuss and work things out for themselves, but when things got sticky, he would step in and pray about it. Many reminisced about going to school together when they were little, about the invisible borders that rose up between them and didn't allow them to cross that line. They began to remember the things they did as youngsters."

Twilight Bey, an architect of the Los Angeles truce and a member of the Bloods gang, recalls the countless Wednesdays at Brown's house. "Sometimes there was so much metal [weaponry] that if you melted it down it would become a tanker," he says. "But it worked so that eventually there was no need to bring metal to the house. There [we could see that] this person feels and hurts in the same way I do, and the only way to stop the pain is to stop hurting each other. Young men expressed their anger and pain but also expressed that they would try to communicate. Some of us have found some of our closest friends to be people from the other side."

The thrust of the truce discussions was often political. Bey says the young men would "talk about what was happening in our community and what it would take to change it. That's where we came down to empowerment and the Maer-I-Can skills program [a system promoted by Jim Brown]: it's about life-management skills, decision making, emotional control, job search and retention, drug abuse."

Why Young People Join Truces

We don't set up the gang truce. The young people have to set it up themselves. We assist them and we try to give them some support. The empowerment lies in them being part of it. We think it is very critical to fight the "do it for me" mentality. Our slogan is, "We won't do it for you, but we will do it with you."

There are a number of reasons why young people start getting active in supporting the truce. Some circumstances include the death of a friend or family member, facing a long jail sentence, or as a result of their own direct experience at the hands of the police. Sometimes they come to the conclusion that they have played a negative role in the community and they want to change that. They begin to see that there is a viable alternative to their existing lifestyle. Others get involved as a result of changes in their personal lives: having children, getting into a stable relationship, finding a job that they like. These changes give a young person something to live and work for and can motivate people to move in a different direction.

Michael Zinzun, interviewed by Nancy Stein, *Social Justice*, Winter 1997.

"We were talking about disenfranchised youth, economic depravation, estrangement from society, the unfair laws from capitalism—all issues that affected us directly," he says. "This is a time we were asked questions that weren't ever asked before: What are we going to do to change our situation? Do we have the power? Of course. Do we have any say on what happens in political arena. What does it take to change things?"

"Jim was a surrogate father," Bey continues. "Jim was a man who spoke the truth. He never sold us any false dreams, any false hopes. He told us things that might have hurt in the beginning but were all good in the end. He told us we were predators in our own communities, that we did things that weren't right. He told us no one's going to pay us to stop killing each other, that we had to change our own routines. He was always very direct, but if you needed his help, he was there."

Truce activists in the Latino community use similar methods to bring gang adversaries together. Daniel "Nane" Alejandrez, director of a national gang peace group called Barrios Unidos, says, "We're seeing a spiritual movement where a lot of Chicano [gang members] are going into the sweat lodge and realizing there's a lot of power in our Native American culture."

The importance of the sweat lodge, he says, has to do with what happens when people gather together: "You connect to people who've been in the same situation, and so you reconnect with yourself. And that's where you get that healing, by connecting to something good within you, in the realization that we're not alone.". . .

Some Truces Fail

No matter how much effort goes into them, some truces just don't hold. The barriers—such as police interference and the lack of economic alternatives—are often too great. Ironically, in some areas where truces have successfully ended random killings and youth gang violence, gang members have gone into drug dealing instead.

Ray Balberon of the Real Alternatives Project (RAP) in San Francisco has seen local truces come and go. A major culprit for the failure, he believes, is the economic reality of the ghetto. "Calling for a truce without an alternative is difficult," he says. "Do we have resources to deliver? Employment? Schools?"

A truce that doesn't include ways to deliver jobs, counseling and other services to the community can even backfire. Sgt. Robert Montague of the Philadelphia police department remembers the truce 15 years ago involving the Zulu Nation, a gigantic Black gang whose territory covered three square miles of housing projects. Homicides fell significantly after a truce was signed, but then crack entered the scene. "These guys started dealing drugs, so the gang dissolved. Their main purpose had been fighting each other, but when they got involved in drugs, they turned their attention to drugs and stopped thinking about each other. Now Philadelphia doesn't have a youth-gang problem at all—we have drug gangs."

Likewise, Chicago's truces "haven't affected the drug dealing," according to Frank Chávez of the Chicago chapter of Barrios Unidos. "As a matter of fact, a truce can mean an opportunity for more people to start [dealing] narcotics. A truce stops the violence—not necessarily the drug dealing."

Internal and External Threats

The writer Luis Rodríguez worked with Chávez on a truce between Rogers Park and Logan Square gangs. But he says he's very suspicious of recent accusations of drug dealing among gangs who became politicized. He told *Third Force* that Chicago's Gangster Disciples, who had formed a truce with the Vice Lords and became Growth and Development, a political action group, was indicted as a front for drug dealing, even though the group had organized a march last year for jobs. "You get the sense [that] the cops move in on people only when they're becoming more socially, culturally and politically viable," Rodríguez says. "When the group called itself the Gangster Disciples, they did drugs, but the government never moved in on them."

The truces are threatened internally as well. Balberon explains: "Some gangs at times do want a truce, but not as a whole. A faction of the gang wants it, another doesn't. The issue may even cause a split and start internal fighting." Such has been the case in Chicago, known as one of the most violent cities in the country. Sgt. Luis Lara of the Chicago Police Department's Gang Crimes Unit believes the nature of

151

youth gangs conspires against peace. "It's too wide spectrum," he says. "There's older ones trying to make peace, [but the] peewees are not listening to them at all and are still wanting to make a name for themselves."

But according to Sadicki, police who are distrustful of truces are often a main factor in their breakdown. "I've seen the police perpetuate conflict in one way or another in Kansas City, Los Angeles and Minnesota," Sadicki says.

It also doesn't help when police crackdowns eliminate truce-oriented gang leadership. For example, when much of the leadership of the Mexican Mafia was swept into Pelican Bay State Prison between 1990 and 1993, these individuals were replaced by people who didn't agree with the peace process. The result was turmoil on California streets.

The Truce Is Just the First Step

Peace by itself doesn't bring about a change in the social conditions that lead to gangs or even change the way the gangs operate. Long Beach's Asian Boyz are staying true to their truce with the Mexican American East Side Longos. However, they continue to extort money from their own community and local businesses. Professor Riposo says the truce did nothing about the "multiple marginality—the racism, the class oppression, the poverty and unemployment that so clearly correlates with gangs. The economic plan the city has in place won't change gang behavior because the city is focused on downtown [economic development]."

Rick Cevallos, a Barrios Unidos organizer in Venice, California, agrees. Gang truces, he says, can't cure the social illness that innercity kids suffer on a daily basis. "A truce only says that these communities got together, that they're trying to stop the violence and are looking for alternatives," Cevallos says. "And that's all that is." Poverty-stricken communities need infusions of economic aid, job training programs and other assistance on a level that only government can provide, he says.

But this hasn't stopped truce supporters from making their contributions. Zinzun, of Los Angeles' Communities in Support of a Gang Truce, is too busy to talk for long on the phone—he's got a rally to organize, police abuse to denounce, a vision to set down on paper. "We need to expand the truce," he says, warning that he can only answer five minutes' worth of questions. His group shows videos, distributes literature and has a speakers' bureau with both Latino and Black orators. It also trains gang members in pest control, providing those interested with two months' worth of supplies and equipping them with a marketing plan; 50 gang members have been trained so far. There's also a free silk-screening class that gives kids an opportunity to create clothing to sell in stores and trade at local swap meets.

Zinzun constantly networks with others in the truce movement: Hands across Watts, the Peace and Freedom Party, the clergy, unions, teachers and probation officers all over the country. He wants to establish a national electoral campaign focused on solving urban problems. "I don't want us to promote some sorry-ass politician like Jesse Jackson—we're talking about seizing the agenda," he says. "This is new, it's not intended to promote these fools but to bring in fresh blood. We want to think about long-term politics." On that note, he's got to run.

Individual Contributions

Barrios Unidos' Alejandrez is also a busy man. He's devising ways to yank loose some money from the federal government for violence prevention and economic development. "We must take it upon ourselves to develop barrio enterprise zones, in conjunction with business, the community and the churches," he says.

Already he's done a lot. Barrios Unidos in Santa Cruz is training barrio kids in computer literacy in the César Chávez School of Social Change. One of the computer instructors, a Chicano, is only 12 years old. The organization's Kids Club, an after-school tutoring program for latchkey or neglected children from the projects, gives gang-bangers a chance to be caretakers and leaders. New Barrios Unidos chapters are sprouting up around the country, especially in the Southwest.

The fruits of gang peace are perhaps most evident on the individual level. Take Twilight Bey. His pager beeps often—one time when I spoke with him it was a business interested in selling to the Black community that wanted his assessment on what it should know to keep customers happy. Bey is now a private community consultant; he does presentations at schools to explain Maer-I-Can, the program used in the Watts truce that teaches self esteem and self-determination; and he's ready to run for elected office. "Instead of banging on a negative note," he says, "I've found other ways of getting my kicks."

Periodical Bibliography

The following articles have been selected to supplement the diverse views presented in this chapter. Addresses are provided for periodicals not indexed in the *Readers' Guide to Periodical Literature*, the *Alternative Press Index*, the *Social Sciences Index*, or the *Index to Legal Periodicals and Books*.

Tiffany Danitz	"Keeping Kids Out of Gangs," *Insight on the News*, July 6–13, 1998. Available from 3600 New York Ave. NE, Washington, DC 20002.
Gary Delgado	"Warriors for Peace: Stopping Youth Violence with Barrios Unidos," *Colorlines*, Winter 1999.
Debra Dickerson	"Cease-Fire in Simple City," *U.S. News & World Report*, March 16, 1998.
Craig Donegan	"Preventing Juvenile Crime," *CQ Researcher*, March 15, 1996. Available from 1414 22nd St. NW, Washington, DC 20037.
Ted Gest	"A Taxpayer's Guide to Crime and Punishment," *U.S. News & World Report*, April 21, 1997.
Juvenile Justice Update	"What Works in Preventing Youth Crime: Systematic Assessment Provides Some Surprises," October/November 1997. Available from Civic Research Institute, 4490 U.S. Route 27, PO Box 585, Kingston, NJ 08528.
Greg Michie	"A Teacher Reflects on Kids and Gangs: 'You Gotta Be Hard,'" *Rethinking Schools*, Winter 1997/1998.
Carol Ann Morrow	"Gang Priest," *St. Anthony Messenger*, August 1999. Available from 1615 Republic St., Cincinnati, OH 45210-1298.
Janet Patti and Linda Lantieri	"The War for Peace," *Professional Counselor*, August 1997. Available from 3201 Southwest 15th St., Deerfield Beach, FL 33442-8190.
Colin Powell	"I Wasn't Left to Myself," *Newsweek*, April 27, 1998.
Ron Stodghill II	"In the Line of Fire," *Time*, April 20, 1998.
Andrew P. Thomas	"From Gangs to God," *Wall Street Journal*, October 23, 1998.

Quint C. Thurman, Andrew L. Giacomazzi, Michael D. Reisig, and David G. Mueller — "Community-Based Gang Prevention and Intervention: An Evaluation of the Neutral Zone," *Crime & Delinquency*, April 1996. Available from Sage Publications, 2455 Teller Rd., Thousand Oaks, CA 91320.

Robert L. Woodson — "A D.C. Neighborhood's Hard-Won Peace," *Wall Street Journal*, February 21, 1997.

Robert L. Woodson — "Reclaiming the Lives of Young People," *USA Today*, September 1997.

For Further Discussion

Chapter 1

1. Lewis Yablonsky asserts that gang members often suffer emotional problems, ranging from parental abuse to depression. However, many children face similar circumstances and do not turn to violence. Why do you think some youth with these problems join gangs, while others do not? Explain your answer.

2. Isis Sapp-Grant is a former gang member and Dale Greer is an inmate. Do you think this makes their explanations on what factors lead to gang involvement more compelling than viewpoints written by authors who are researchers of, but not participants in, criminal life? Why or why not?

3. Music has often been accused of inciting violence, whether it is Marilyn Manson after the Columbine shootings in 1999 or gangster rap, as in the viewpoint by Rick Landre, Mike Miller, and Dee Porter. However, other musical genres, such as country music, are not blamed even though they also sometimes have violent lyrics. Why do you think some bands and artists are accused of encouraging violence while others are not? Do you think that music is a factor in gang violence? Explain your answers.

Chapter 2

1. Stereotyping is a recurrent theme in this chapter's viewpoints, as the authors explain how certain bias can lead to some groups being labeled gangs while others, though committing similar crimes, are not. After reading these viewpoints, do you believe an accurate definition of gangs can be formulated, or will any definition be marred by stereotypes? Explain your answer.

2. Gini Sikes explains that while girls join gangs because they seek acceptance and want to be valued, they are often treated poorly by their male counterparts. If her assessment is accurate, why do you think girls continue to participate in gangs? How do you think the existence of female gangs would be altered if they were not auxiliaries to male gangs? Explain your answers.

3. Tim Wise writes in a sarcastic tone throughout his viewpoint, using phrases such as "These are the beautiful people. They never do anything wrong." Do you think that Wise's writing style improves or detracts from his argument? Why or why not?

Chapter 3

1. Joseph Marshall Jr. and Lonnie Wheeler compare the situation in America's cities to that of the Middle East. Do you believe the authors' comparison is an effective way to highlight the problem of gang violence and what should be done to prevent it? Why or why not?

2. Richard K. Willard and David Cole disagree as to whether inner city residents support loitering laws. Whose argument do you find more convincing and why?

3. The authors in this chapter evaluate various approaches to reducing gang violence. Which, if any, of these methods do you think would be most successful? What other steps do you think the criminal justice system could take? Explain your answers.

Chapter 4

1. Arturo Hernandez and Elizabeth J. Swasey disagree as to whether schools can institute programs that will reduce gang violence. How do the school programs they discuss differ? Do you agree with Swasey when she argues that the after-school programs are a failure because one or two students who participate in the programs commit crimes? Explain your answers.

2. Rick Landre, Mike Miller, and Dee Porter contend that legal pressure might need to be placed on parents who are unwilling to participate in antigang efforts. Do you agree with this view? Why or why not?

3. After reading the viewpoints in this chapter, who do you think can best end the problem of gang violence—youth, their families, or all of society? Are there any other alternatives that you feel may be effective in reducing gang violence? Explain your answers.

Organizations to Contact

The editors have compiled the following list of organizations concerned with issues debated in this book. The descriptions are derived from materials provided by the organizations. All have publications or information available for interested readers. The list was compiled on the date of publication of the present volume; the information provided here may change. Be aware that many organizations take several weeks or longer to respond to inquiries, so allow as much time as possible.

American Civil Liberties Union (ACLU)

125 Broad St., 18th Floor, New York, NY 10004
(212) 549-2500 • fax: (212) 549-2646
e-mail: aclu@aclu.org • website: www.aclu.org

The ACLU is a national organization that works to defend Americans' civil rights as guaranteed by the U.S. Constitution. It opposes curfew laws for juveniles and others and seeks to protect the public-assembly rights of gang members or people associated with gangs. The ACLU publishes the biannual newsletter *Civil Liberties*.

California Youth Authority Office of Prevention and Victim Services (OPVS)

Office of Prevention and Victim Services
California Youth Authority
4241 Williamsbourgh Dr., Suite 214, Sacramento, CA 95823
(916) 262-1392
e-mail: klowe@cya.ca.gov
website: www.cya.ca.gov/organization/opvs.html

The Office of Prevention and Victim Services coordinates a wide range of victims services and administers several programs, including the Gang Violence Reduction Programs (GVRP). OPVS staff serve as consultants to local delinquency prevention programs and provide staff support for the State Commission on Juvenile Justice, Crime, and Delinquency Prevention. Its publications include the monthly newsletter *CYA Today*.

Center for the Community Interest (CCI)

114 E. 32nd St., Suite 604, New York, NY 10016
(212) 689-6080 • fax: (212) 689-6370
e-mail: mail@communityinterest.org
website: www.communityinterest.org

The Center for the Community Interest (CCI) is a national organization that speaks out on crime and quality-of-life issues. CCI supports policies that strike a balance between rights and responsibilities and defends those policies when demands for civil liberties are carried to unreasonable extremes. Publications include the backgrounder "Juvenile Curfews."

Gang and Youth Crime Prevention Program (GYCPP)
Ministry of Attorney General, Community Justice Branch
207-815 Hornby St., Vancouver, BC V6Z 2E6 Canada
(604) 660-2605 • hotline: (800) 680-4264 (British Columbia only)
fax: (604) 775-2674

This program works with government ministries, police, public agencies, community-based organizations, and youth in order to raise awareness, and reduce the incidence, of gang- and youth-related crime and violence. GYCPP maintains a youth violence directory, conducts community forums and school workshops, creates videos, and publishes a set of booklets on Canada's criminal justice system.

The Heritage Foundation
214 Massachusetts Ave. NE, Washington, DC 20002
(202) 546-4400 • fax: (202) 546-8328

The Heritage Foundation is a conservative public policy research institute. It advocates tougher sentences and the construction of more prisons as means to reduce crime. The foundation publishes papers, including "How State and Local Officials Can Combat Violent Juvenile Crime," and the quarterly journal *Policy Review*, which occasionally contains articles addressing juvenile crime.

Join Together
441 Stuart St., Boston, MA 02116
(617) 437-1500 • fax: (617) 437-9394
e-mail: info@jointogether.org
website: www.jointogether.org

Join Together, a project of the Boston University School of Public Health, is an organization that serves as a national resource for communities working to reduce substance abuse and gun violence. Its publications include a quarterly newsletter.

Milton S. Eisenhower Foundation
1660 L St. NW, Suite 200, Washington, DC 20036
(202) 429-0440
website: www.eisenhowerfoundation.org

The foundation consists of individuals dedicated to reducing crime in inner-city neighborhoods through community programs.

It believes that more federally funded programs such as Head Start and Job Corps would improve education and job opportunities for youths, thus reducing juvenile crime and violence. The foundation's publications include the reports "To Establish Justice, to Ensure Domestic Tranquility: A Thirty Year Update of the National Commission on the Causes and Prevention of Violence," and "Youth Investment and Police Mentoring," and the monthly newsletter *Challenges from Within*.

National Council on Crime and Delinquency (NCCD)
1970 Broadway, Suite 500, Oakland, CA 94612
(510) 208-0500 • fax: (510) 208-0511
e-mail: rjohnson@itis.com • website: www.nccd-crc.org

The NCCD is composed of corrections specialists and others interested in the juvenile justice system and the prevention of crime and delinquency. It advocates community-based treatment programs rather than imprisonment for delinquent youths. It opposes placing minors in adult jails and executing those who commit capital offenses before the age of eighteen. Publications include the quarterlies *Crime and Delinquency* and *Journal of Research in Crime and Delinquency* and the papers "The Impact of the Justice System on Serious, Violent, and Chronic Juvenile Offenders," and "Images and Reality: Juvenile Crime, Youth Violence, and Public Policy."

National Crime Prevention Council (NCPC)
1000 Connecticut Ave. NW, 13th Floor, Washington, DC 20036
(202) 466-6272 • fax: (202) 296-1356

NCPC provides training and technical assistance to groups and individuals interested in crime prevention. It advocates job training and recreation programs as means to reduce youth crime and violence. The council, which sponsors the Take a Bite Out of Crime campaign, publishes the books *Preventing Violence: Program Ideas and Examples* and *350 Tested Strategies to Prevent Crime*, the booklet "Making Children, Families, and Communities Safer From Violence," and the newsletter *Catalyst*, which is published ten times a year.

National Institute of Justice (NIJ)
810 Seventh St. NW, Washington, DC 20531
(202) 307-2942 • fax: (202) 307-6394
website: www.ojp.usdoj.gov/nij

NIJ is the primary federal sponsor of research on crime and its control. It sponsors research efforts through grants and contracts that are carried out by universities, private institutions, and state and local agencies. Its publications include "Comparing the Criminal Behavior of Youth Gangs and At-Risk Youths," "High School Youths, Weapons, and Violence: A National Survey," and "Youth Afterschool Programs and Law Enforcement."

National School Safety Center (NSSC)
141 Duesenberg Dr., Suite 11, Westlake Village, CA 91362
(805) 373-9977 • fax: (805) 373-9277
e-mail: info@nssc1.org • website: www.nssc1.org

Part of Pepperdine University, the center is a research organization that studies school crime and violence, including gang and hate crimes, and that provides technical assistance to local school systems. NSSC believes that teacher training is an effective way of reducing juvenile crime. It publishes the booklet *Gangs in Schools: Breaking Up Is Hard to Do*, the *School Safety Update* newsletter, published nine times a year, and the resource papers "Safe Schools Overview" and "Weapons in Schools."

Office of Juvenile Justice and Delinquency Prevention (OJJDP)
810 Seventh St. NW, Washington, DC 20531
(202) 307-5911 • fax: (202) 307-2093
e-mail: askjj@ojp.usdoj.gov • website: http://ojjdp.ncjrs.org

As the primary federal agency charged with monitoring and improving the juvenile justice system, the OJJDP develops and funds programs on juvenile justice. Among its goals are the prevention and control of illegal drug use and serious crime by juveniles. Through its Juvenile Justice Clearinghouse, the OJJDP distributes fact sheets, the annual *Youth Gang Survey* and reports such as "Youth Gangs: An Overview" and "Gang Suppression and Intervention: Community Models."

Teens Against Gang Violence (TAGV)
2 Moody St., Dorchester, MA 02124
(617) 282-9659 • fax: (617) 282-9659
e-mail: teensagv@aol.com • website: http://tagv.org

Teens Against Gang Violence, or TAGV, is a volunteer, community-based, teen peer leadership program. TAGV distinguishes between gangs that are nonviolent and those that participate in violence. Through presentations and workshops, the organization educates teens, parents, schools and community groups on violence, guns, and drug prevention.

Youth Crime Watch of America (YCWA)
9300 S. Dadeland Blvd., Suite 100, Miami, FL 33156
(305) 670-2409 • fax: (305) 670-3805
e-mail: ycwa@ycwa.org • website: www.ycwa.org
YCWA is a nonprofit, student-led organization that promotes crime and drug prevention programs in communities and schools throughout the United States. Member-students at the elementary and secondary level help raise others' awareness concerning alcohol and drug abuse, crime, gangs, guns, and the importance of staying in school. Strategies include organizing student assemblies and patrols, conducting workshops, and challenging students to become personally involved in preventing crime and violence. YCWA publishes the quarterly newsletter *National Newswatch* and the *Community-Based Youth Crime Watch Program Handbook*.

Bibliography of Books

S. Beth Atkin — *Voices from the Streets: Young Former Gang Members Tell Their Stories*. Boston: Little, Brown, 1996.

Curtis W. Branch and Paul Pedersen, eds. — *Adolescent Gangs: Old Issues, New Approaches*. Philadelphia: Brunner/Mazel, 1999.

Douglas Century — *Street Kingdom: Five Years Inside the Franklin Avenue Posse*. New York: Warner, 1999.

Meda Chesney-Lind and John M. Hagedorn, eds. — *Female Gangs in America: Essays on Girls, Gangs, and Gender*. Chicago: Lake View, 1999.

Ko-Lin Chin — *Chinatown Gangs: Extortion, Enterprise, and Ethnicity*. New York: Oxford University Press, 1996.

Herbert C. Covey, Scott Menard, and Robert J. Franzese — *Juvenile Gangs*. Springfield, IL: Charles C. Thomas, 1997.

G. David Curry and Scott H. Decker — *Confronting Gangs: Crime and Community*. Los Angeles: Roxbury, 1998.

Scott H. Decker and Barrik Van Winkle — *Life in the Gang: Family, Friends, and Violence*. Cambridge, England: Cambridge University Press, 1996.

Mark S. Fleisher — *Dead End Kids: Gang Girls and the Boys They Know*. Madison: University of Wisconsin Press, 1998.

James Garbarino — *Lost Boys: Why Our Sons Turn Violent and How We Can Save Them*. New York: Free, 1999.

Gus Gedatus — *Gangs and Violence*. Mankato, MN: LifeMatters, 2000.

Arnold P. Goldstein and Donald W. Kodluboy — *Gangs in Schools: Signs, Symbols, and Solutions*. Champaign, IL: Research, 1998.

Vernon T. Harlan — *Youth Street Gangs: Breaking the Gangs Cycle in Urban America*. San Francisco: Austin & Winfield, 1997.

Arturo Hernandez — *Peace in the Streets: Breaking the Cycle of Gang Violence*. Washington, DC: Child Welfare League of America, 1998.

James C. Howell — *Juvenile Justice and Youth Violence*. Thousand Oaks, CA: Sage, 1997.

C. Ronald Huff, ed. — *Gangs in America*. Thousand Oaks, CA: Sage, 1999.

Lonnie Jackson — *Gangbusters: Strategies for Prevention and Intervention.* Lanham, MD: American Correctional Association, 1998.

Karen L. Kinnear — *Gangs: A Reference Handbook.* Santa Barbara, CA: ABC-CLIO, 1996.

Rick Landre, Mike Miller, and Dee Porter — *Gangs: A Handbook for Community Awareness.* New York: Facts On File, 1997.

Joseph Marshall Jr. and Lonnie Wheeler — *Street Soldier: One Man's Struggle to Save a Generation—One Life at a Time.* New York: Bantam Doubleday Dell, 1996.

G. Larry Mays, ed. — *Gangs and Gang Behavior.* Chicago: Nelson-Hall, 1997.

Maryann Miller — *Coping with Weapons and Violence at School and on Your Streets.* New York: Rosen, 1999.

Dennise Orlando-Morningstar — *Street Gangs.* Washington, DC: Federal Judicial Center, 1997.

Susan A. Phillips — *Wallbangin': Graffiti and Gangs in L.A.* Chicago: University of Chicago Press, 1999.

Joseph Rodriguez, Rubén Martínez, and Luis J. Rodríguez — *East Side Stories: Gang Life in East L.A.* New York: PowerHouse, 1998.

Steven L. Sachs — *Street Gang Awareness: A Resource Guide for Parents and Professionals.* Minneapolis: Fairview, 1997.

Eric C. Schneider — *Vampires, Dragons, and Egyptian Kings: Youth Gangs in Postwar New York.* Princeton, NJ: Princeton University Press, 1999.

Randall G. Shelden, Sharon K. Tracy, and William B. Brown — *Youth Gangs in American Society.* Belmont, CA: Wadsworth, 1996.

Gini Sikes — *8 Ball Chicks: A Year in the Violent World of Girl Gangsters.* New York: Doubleday, 1997.

Ben Sonder — *Gangs.* New York: Benchmark, 1996.

Margi Trapani — *Working Together Against Gang Violence.* New York: Rosen, 1996.

Al Valdez — *Gangs: A Guide to Understanding Street Gangs.* San Clemente, CA: Lawtech, 1997.

Ved Varma, ed. — *Violence in Children and Adolescents.* London: Jessica Kingsley, 1997.

Liza Vertinsky — *A Law and Economic Approach to Criminal Gangs.* Aldershot, England: Ashgate, 1999.

Valerie Wiener   *Winning the War Against Youth Gangs: A Guide for Teens, Families, and Communities.* Westport, CT: Greenwood, 1999.

Lewis Yablonsky   *Gangsters: Fifty Years of Madness, Drugs, and Death on the Streets of America.* New York: New York University Press, 1997.

Index